Christian Approaches to Therapeutic Parenting

Help for the Hurting Child

LARRY E. BANTA, MD FAPA

ISBN: 978-1-990695-55-1 (Paperback)
978-1-990695-62-9 (Hardback)
978-1-990695-61-2 (E-book)

BookSide Press
877-741-8091
www.booksidepress.com
orders@booksidepress.com

Contents

The US Review of Books

Professional Reviews for the People

Help for the Hurting Child: Christian Approaches to Therapeutic Parenting by *Larry E. Banta, MD*
Reviewed by: **Mihir Shah**

"During various stages of development, there are special times when the child, or even the adult, is more vulnerable to the effects of trauma."

Well researched and comprehensive, Banta's work is a fusion of his experiences and deeper probings as they pertain to paving a healthy and functional pathway for children who have been displaced from their original families for one reason or another. What gives the author's work even greater credence and legitimacy is the firsthand accounts and interactions he has had with those working directly with the children, from foster parents to orphanages. Piecing together the three core topics of psychology, psychiatry, and religion, the work is a bona fide guide toward providing a holistic and therapeutic game plan to develop the child.

More than anything else, the text focuses on helping authority figures—the stewards of our children's future—avoid the constant disruptions in their developmental experience that have so tragically become a trademark of well-known adoptive placement systems like foster care. To this end, Banta does an exceptional job of helping educate the masses on acquiring an understanding of child development, both the necessity of it and the science behind it. In essence, his theory is that adults first must be committed to the process of child development with Christian approaches before the child can be expected to exhibit that same level of commitment to faith and the family system.

The author takes incredibly complex topics and finds a way to simplify them so even the layman can understand. In particular, explaining psychological concepts like extinction, withdrawals, and mental illness can be rife with confusing theories. However, he filters out the complexities using scripture and examples and leaves only the substance for the reader to digest. The holistic approach to development is predicated upon balancing all aspects of humanity, from spirituality and physical health to mental and emotional well-being. If any of these core categories are off-kilter, Banta suggests that chaos will ensue and open a path for Satan to enter and corrupt the mind.

Describing a series of systems throughout, Banta emphasizes that positive energy is a prerequisite to establishing healthy growth in a child. Conjure the image of a child who has grown in isolation. It becomes evident that an appropriate level of attachment is necessary, as is the importance of acknowledging that there will be a learning curve with the child. They simply won't mesh seamlessly with an adult's discipline style or even a style that inundates the child with love that often comes across as out of pity. Specifically, the author lays out remnants of a system that can establish and reinforce the attachment with a healing child. In particular, daily and cultural rituals are essential to overall progress.

Perhaps the most intriguing aspect of this roadmap is its ability to highlight development from the entire lifespan of a child from infancy. Undoubtedly, the portion on dreams, especially REM sleep, and understanding the fundamentals of behavior management are the cornerstones of conditioning and psychology as a whole. Conversely, it is not simply the behavior of the child that must be evaluated, but also that of the adult, who must be cognizant of every action and communication and how it could affect the healing child. Above all else, faith in Christ acts as the great equalizer, focusing on unconditional love and forgiveness regardless of the behaviors and the potential shortcomings from the scientific front. Collectively, however, the author's strength lies in the thoroughness of his work and in his ability to weave together science and religion for the betterment of the child.

RECOMMENDED by the US Review

PREFACE

During the past several decades, I have had the opportunity to meet and work with many who have served as foster parents, adoptive parents, house parents in orphanages and children's facilities, administrators of facilities, as well as working directly with several state agencies in Idaho and Nebraska serving children in out-of-home placement. I have trained many workers and administrators over the years but have learned countless lessons from those serving as the caregivers of these special children. With my own background in child and adolescent psychiatry and the experience of working with the special people who dedicated their lives and careers in working with these children, I have been able to compile some material that should be helpful for anyone who is involved with children who are not able to be in their own homes or with their original families.

My strong desire is that this manual would serve as a reference, a starting point, toward continued learning for those in this type of children's ministry. There is always more to know. We must always be looking for better ways to accomplish the important work of helping these children to get a great start in life in spite of the situation that they come from. An important part of any ministry is to be humble enough to learn and profit from the experiences of others. There is good science behind much of what we can use in enhancing this type of ministry.

The science of psychology offers a great deal in terms of understanding what happens in normal and abnormal development. The great work on understanding attachment and how it truly affects the entire course of life has been one of the great discoveries of this field.

The medical specialty of psychiatry has offered some approaches, well studied, as to how to reach these children and to assist them with getting back on a good developmental track to be able to be successful. This includes the judicious use of medication combined with therapeutic approaches shown to be effective in working with children.

Theology is the foundation on which we can discern what is true from the above disciplines and to provide the child with understanding his origin, the true meaning and purpose of life, what is morality, and what is the basis of the rules that we live by. Our belief in the Creator God and His Son Jesus also provides us with the ultimate destiny of life, heaven.

Utilizing the principles above, we can truly help the children to become ***PRODUCTIVE COMMITTED CHRISTIAN ADULTS.***

INTRODUCTION

The primary purpose of this book is to assist those caring for children unable to be with their original parents. There are many reasons this occurs. Some might be truly orphaned, their parents having died from AIDS, Ebola, or another epidemic or because of an accident, war, terrorism, or some other illness or tragedy. Others perhaps come from situations in which original parents or adoptive parents are not able to care for them due to factors related to either the child or parents. Whatever the situation, these children do not have the advantage of living with their original set of parents and are now in some type of alternative home placement.

The placement may be a foster home, adoptive home, orphanage, children's home, residential school, or other type of placement.

The issue of raising children who cannot be with their parents of origin has always been a challenge. As Christians, we are commanded to care for the widows and orphans, as this fulfills true religion:

> Religion that God our Father accepts as pure and faultless is this: to look after orphans and widows in their distress and to keep oneself from being polluted by the world. (James 1:27)

The growing problem of orphaned and abandoned children provides a great challenge for the church today. This was mainly an urban issue for many years, as families from rural areas traveled to urban areas and left their children there when they felt they could no longer care for them. Over the years, I have met many of these children, some as adults. Many had the opportunity of a loving home to grow up in, either through adoption or in a children's home. Some grew up on the street and endured sometimes terrible trauma and loneliness. Now the issue is widespread and can be found just about everywhere, even in the rural communities of African countries or in India, where many ministries are reaching out. In the US, the problem of homeless and abandoned children is growing. Further complicating this issue is the problem of sex trafficking. This is a great opportunity for God's people to provide a special and needed ministry in many different ways.

The concept of parenting is something we learn from our own parents, good or bad. Most of us, Christians in particular, learn to modify our behaviors when we have the desire to improve on the parenting styles of our parents. Otherwise, we generally repeat their errors, often lovingly but unwittingly made, and continue those dysfunctional patterns through yet another generation. Parenting children we procreate is often difficult enough, but choosing the noble task of the ministry to care for children who do not have parents or cannot live with their original parents is a real challenge. It must be done right.

The concept of therapeutic parenting is to accept the challenge of raising children that need more than just parenting. This involves learning how to best deal with sometimes a very damaged, hurting child. Love is not enough, but is a very good start. Approaches need to address the whole child. Psychology and psychiatry have offered much in how to understand and care for the special needs presented. There are many approaches in terms of housing.

One way to care for them is the traditional orphanage or children's home. Many types of children's homes exist throughout the world—some do well, while others do not. The results depend on keeping the right focus in the ministry and developing a program that maintains a healthy environment that successfully addresses physical, spiritual, and mental challenges.

Some orphanages use the model of a "normal" home. A couple, often still raising their own children, will manage a home with twenty or more children often of both sexes and all ages. This works for some, as the outcome is fairly good much of the time. However, some orphaned children have trouble tolerating the idea of someone else representing their mother or father—especially the mother, due to the trauma of having been separated from her, abandoned by her, not protected from abuse by her, abused by her. There is a subconscious tendency for these children to blame the foster or adoptive mother for the situation that left them homeless. They tend to take out the anger of being abandoned, hurt, or betrayed on the nearest representation of a mother, the female in the home. If abuse was perpetrated by a father figure, then anger toward the one representing that role often occurs.

Over the years, after working with various models and consulting with homes in several countries, I've found that an effective model for the many children that must be cared for in an orphanage-type situation is the dormitory model but with very consistent substitute or therapeutic parents. No one is clearly identified as "mother" or "father," but instead often called tutor or aunt/uncle.

Foster homes are one of the more common types of care for these children in many countries. However, many foster homes are run by well-meaning but untrained parents. One of the most serious deficiencies is the lack of understanding of the attachment process. This results in children passing through an average of thirteen homes by the time they reach age eighteen in the US system. This can result in an adult form of attachment disorder in which the person struggles with the ability to form stable relationships. With proper training and supervision, this type of placement could work very well and would be considered the best option pending adoption if the child cannot return to the original home.

Adoptive placement is meant to be more permanent and often starts with a foster care relationship. However, if the adoptive parents are not properly prepared or the child is just too difficult to manage, the adoption can fail with the child ending up in an alternative residential setting and has to endure yet another disruption in their developmental experience.

This is one of the most challenging types of ministries. The energy required, the emotional stress, and the temptations that occur in emotionally vulnerable staff/parents make it a challenge and opportunity to grow spiritually—or alternatively create a situation in which serious spiritual problems can develop.

However, when you see the results—a child following Christ in commitment and baptism, now a grown and productive, committed adult Christian servant whose life was changed during your ministry—the reward is such profound joy, you can hardly stand it!

To effectively minister to these children, we need to understand child development, particularly issues around promoting attachment, as that is the primary job of the caregiver. We also must understand how to deal with behaviors and challenges to authority so we can help them grow. These challenges are important, and our reactions to them can turn them into successful learning and growing experiences…or not. If we sow too much negativity, the harvest is bitterness.

We must also deal with the management of the home. That means developing and maintaining the structure. This requires invested energy. In this manual, you will learn about structure, how to design and maintain the home, and what makes for a successful environment.

We also help you deal with yourself as the caregiver. We want everyone to succeed, so you must keep your life in balance—spiritually, physically, mentally, and emotionally. Still, as you take on the challenges of this type of ministry, always keep in mind that the children are your focus, as their future is in your hands.

To effectively understand how this type of ministry works, you will be first introduced to the very important topic of "systems," how things work when people need to accomplish a task together. Following that, we will look at how to build the structure that will help the children to grow up being secure and healthy. To learn what their lives are like, we will look at the most important issue in development—attachment and how it relates to the rest of these children's lives. This is followed by some basic guidelines on behavior management, discipline, and making disciples by being an example for our children to help them follow Jesus's teachings in their own lives.

Throughout the book, the term *caregiver* has been used to identify those who work directly with the children, be it foster parent, adoptive parent, houseparent, or other term used.

The format is provided in both outline and narrative so that important points can be remembered or quickly found by referring back to a pertinent chapter. The hope and prayer are that this basic instruction book will help you understand how to carry out this ministry effectively and with confidence so that we can meet the goal of guiding children to become productive, committed Christian adults.

1

Systems: How Things Really Work

To fully understand how to create and manage an effective childcare ministry, it is important to understand some basics about how things work in general. Understanding the concept of systems will help you be a better, more productive part of the complete system in which you work.

If you look at a car or motorcycle, you can see that it works only as a result of its collection of parts—all assembled correctly, all doing their assigned tasks, and all working efficiently. If even one part is not working well, the machine might not run, or at least not to its full effect. Each part is important and plays a role. If you neglect your car or motorcycle for a long time, it will eventually fall apart and no longer be useful. If you do not maintain its oil and other fluids, keep it clean, and regularly lubricate the moving parts, it will soon be of no use to you.

Whenever humans gather together to achieve a common purpose or goal, we also are working as a system—a human system, but very much like the mechanical system described above. In a human system, there are the following elements:

Components: These are the parts, all the individuals working in the same system.
Roles: This is similar to a job title.
Responsibilities: What are the particular things each must do to keep things going? This is like a job description.
Relationships: This is about how we respond to one another and defines our connections, whether it be husband-wife, child-parent, child-teacher, child-caregiver, boss-employee, supervisor-worker, administrator-personnel.
Hierarchy: Some roles have more responsibility than others; some are in charge of various aspects of the system to make it work well. Others have the duties assigned by those who are supervising. This extends to the caregiver-child relationship—staffers, not the children, are in charge.

A human system has to be designed to fulfill the function for which it was designed, and all the parts must work together toward a shared goal.

It requires energy to make a system work. Each person doing his or her part instills energy into the system, causing it to become better organized and more functional. Each one taking on his or her role keeps the system from dragging so it operates at optimum levels. Each one in the system who remains predominantly positive in attitude spreads an energy to the rest that is contagious in a good way. If we are avoiding conflict and not being critical, this promotes harmony in the system, and it functions like a well-oiled machine toward accomplishing our purpose.

According to the study of physics, the science of how physical things work, there is a law called the second law of thermodynamics—a big name but a simple concept. What it basically says is that everything tends to become disorganized and goes to chaos. If we do not put energy into something, it will proceed on a path to self-destruction. This is true for your car or motorcycle, as well as for your house, church, school, or childcare ministry.

An abandoned barn, uncared for falls apart

As a part of the system, you must define your roles and responsibilities. This is often done with a job description, helping you to define what it is that you do as your part. Learn your role well. Completing your role, fulfilling your tasks in a way that brings honor to God, will keep the system working well. Encouraging others in their roles also adds energy to the system and causes it to work better.

> Whatever you do, work at it with all your heart, as working for the Lord, not for human masters.
>
> —Colossians 3:23

1917 Craftsman home, excellent condition, cared for over generations.

Doing it with heart, putting your whole self into the ministry, will produce the success that is needed. For the system to work well and harmoniously, it needs to have a defined goal and purpose. The main goal of a childcare ministry is to "produce productive, committed Christian adults." Anything we do while focusing on that goal will help to bring it about. Ask yourself the following questions:

In your childcare ministry:

1. Am I part of the system? If we are working with the children in any role, we are a part of the larger system.
2. What is my role? Houseparent, caregiver, teacher, administrator, supervisor…
3. What are my responsibilities? Provide direct care to the children, which involves many tasks, or maybe supervise and train those in the direct care roles, or run the ministry, making sure there is enough food, personnel, funds, physical plant, to meet the needs of the children to fulfill the goals of the ministry

4. To whom do I report? Who is my supervisor? Making sure of the line of authority and always staying within my role and responsibilities and utilizing the proper hierarchy when needed.
5. What is the goal of the ministry? Generally, to produce productive Christian adults.
6. Is the ministry fulfilling its purpose? Always be thinking about the purpose and goals so that you are doing your part to that end.
7. Do I put positive energy in, or am I sapping the energy in the system? Positive energy to keep the system running, or negative energy that slows everything down and makes the system non-productive.

If you are a foster or adoptive parent:

8. Am I part of the system? Active parenting only, no passive parenting allowed!
9. What is my role? Mother, father, brother, sister, grandparent, foster child?
10. What are my responsibilities? To parent, to be a good brother or sister, grandparent, in-home helper, or a child in the family, fulfilling that role, not trying to be the parent.
11. How can I best carry out those responsibilities? Am I confident and trained to do what I need to do?
12. How do I relate to others in the system? How are we getting along, arguing, disagreeing, or pulling together for the good of the children?
13. What is my ultimate goal as I minister to these children? Make them obey or develop them into productive Christian adults?

Positive Energy: Fulfilling your role, honoring the hierarchy, treating others with respect, encouraging others, keeping yourself healthy in body, mind, and spirit. **Negative Energy:** Arguments, selfishness, authoritarian approach (my way or the highway), putting down others, criticizing without providing positive encouragement, disrespecting hierarchy, gossiping, being a passive parent (just letting the kids raise themselves), not staying healthy in body, mind, or spirit (not keeping up on your own faith). This will lead to gradual destruction of the system and produce adults not ready for the world, destined to fail.

As an integral part of the system, you must constantly examine yourself to see if you are fulfilling your roles and responsibilities and supporting others in fulfilling theirs. If, in addition, you can be a positive and encouraging influence on your coworkers, other family members, you are fulfilling your part *and* adding positive energy and organization to the system. Search your heart before God to make sure you are contributing to the system's success.

Understanding of these basic principles should encourage us to do our best in the system.

So now understanding that we work together as a system to fulfill God's purpose in this ministry, we now need to see how to actually build the system and structure necessary. We will start with understanding how to structure the home so the system works. Maintaining structure requires positive energy.

Keep in mind that everything tends toward chaos, and Satan wants to help it go that way! God's plan is harmony and integrity. He will keep it going that way as long as you keep your focus on Him.

Notes

2

Creating a Successful Home:Structure

To design the proper foundation to run a home, we must have what is called ***structure***. This is like the skeleton or inner workings. It is within this framework that the home operates. Without this structure the home nothing more than a collection of people living in chaos.

What Is Structure?

A structured home has the following qualities:

Consistency
Predictability
Security
Positive Relationships
Healthy Growth and Development

Let's take a look at the characteristics:

Consistency means events and daily activities are generally by routine, on time, and expected—the day has some sort of regular pattern. Things occur, most of the time, in a manner of ***Predictability***. There is a sense of ***Security*** since the patterns allow the children to be comfortable and know what to expect. Due to the fact that things are organized and arranged in a secure way, this in turn allows ***Positive Relationships*** to develop. From this foundation, the child feels safe and experiences ***Healthy Growth and Development***. A major goal of any work with children is to put them back on track developmentally.

Important Concepts

- The family is a system.
- All systems tend toward chaos.
- Energy is required to maintain system integrity or wholeness.
- System integrity begins with the structure.
- Structure is what we do to allow the system to fulfill its purpose.
- The purpose of the Christian family system is to produce healthy, committed, productive, Christian adults who will continue the process.

Recalling the basics of "systems" theory in the first lesson, we can see that the family is a *system*. As such, left on its own without conscious care, it will tend to disorganize and fall apart much the same as an old car left out in the weather or an old neglected barn no longer used. To make the system work, energy is needed. This reverses the tendency toward chaos, serving to develop and maintain *integrity*. Integrity is oneness, wholeness—all parts of the system operating together and well, allowing the machine or system to function properly to fulfill its purpose.

By maintaining structure, we then maintain system integrity. Structure creates the environment in which the system can function. Since all systems have a purpose, the family system can then generate its product—committed, productive Christian adults. When the system is not functioning, the product is destructive rather than constructive. Our job as caretakers is to keep the system running smoothly.

What Does Proper Structure Do?

- ***A child raised in an organized family system learns how to properly manage himself in the world.***
- ***He gains moral grounding, learns the ability to be patient and tolerate delayed gratification, and is less likely to be impulsive and hyperactive.***
- ***He acquires drive and motivation.***
- ***He is more likely to have healthy biological rhythms.***
- ***There is likely to be better control of emotions.***
- ***He will likely have clear understanding and respect of proper boundaries.***

Children coming from chaotic or abusive backgrounds often lack proper tracts in the brain for modulating biorhythms and emotional control. When we think of what chaos and inattention produce, we can imagine that one growing up with that would learn to be chaotic and without his or her own *internal* structure. This produces a poor moral foundation. "I want what I want right now, no delays." The result is also one who cannot control impulses and is more hyperactive. As family structure falls apart, we see a great increase in children with behavior problems. These children also lack future orientation—that is, they do not dream of the future, plan ahead, or think about consequences. Emotions tend to either be flat and unexpressive or without proper context and boundaries. The children are more likely to exhibit symptoms often thought to be from major mental illness (sometimes this is the case, but not always).

The sense of boundaries is taught within the context of structure. Without such, it is hard to know what the rules are. So looking at the systems that seem to be affected by lack of structure, could it be that perhaps structure affects brain development? That is, indeed, the case. External structure produces internal structure. This is an important concept to remember.

External Structure Produces Internal Structure

- ***External structure will gradually become internalized as the child lives within and responds to the system.***
- ***The process of internalizing structure allows for the development of the missing tracts.***
- ***All learning produces new connections or tracts in the brain.***

Learning new things changes the structure of the brain by promoting the development of new tracts, like wires, between various areas of the brain so the person is thus able to act differently. Without structure, children do not have the proper tracts and connections in the brain to modulate emotions and behaviors or even the biological rhythms—when to eat, sleep, go to the bathroom, and so forth.

As the child lives within the structure, the external gradually becomes internal. The structure promotes tracts, new learning, and change in how the child operates. The longer the structure remains in place and the more consistent it is, the more consistent tract development is.

Understanding what ***structure* is,** and how we can create it and maintain it, is a very important part of providing care for these children. The concept of the home as a system helps us understand how we can create the needed structure. The structure of the home includes the following key elements:

- Discipline
- Scheduling
- Rituals
- Boundaries
- Hierarchy
- Roles and Responsibilities

Now we'll take a closer look at each of these key elements.

Discipline

- **Teach what is good and proper, at every chance we get.**
- **Apply consequences to behavior that are consistent, appropriate to the situation, just, non-abusive, and understandable to the child.**
- **Discipline must be kept positive, as much as possible.**
- **Pointing out what is incorrect or inappropriate provides opportunities to quickly turn the focus on correct, appropriate behaviors.**
- **It is essential to look for *teachable moments.***
- **Catching them being good helps to provide positive affirmation.**

Before we can teach what is proper, we must have a foundation of morality that comes from the Word of God. If we lack understanding of His word, we do not ourselves have the fundamentals to pass on to the children. There would be no basis on which to make any moral decisions. Morality would be based on our own human ideas, which are highly subject to change!

It takes energy to be vigilant, to notice when things are not right and make adjustments, to provide guidance, and to consistently manage consequences through to completion As we apply consequences, we must always think about what we are doing:

What is the goal of the consequence?
To teach?
To cause pain and affliction?
To get revenge for something the child did against me?

Always, the goal must be to teach and train. This is why sometimes we need to back off and consider the circumstances and think before taking action. Maybe we could ask advice of others or, better yet, turn to God in a peaceful prayer for guidance, so our reaction does not promote negativity and make things worse. Consequences must be consistently applied, appropriate to the situation, and have the *goal of training the child.*

To understand the purpose of discipline, we need to understand the concept of discipling—that is, helping out children become followers of Jesus. Always keep in mind the goal of producing productive adult Christians. Are the consequences you are applying likely to draw the children closer to God or to push them away from Him? Look forward to moments of discipline as *teachable moments*, when a positive influence can have a potent effect.

Also look for *teachable moments* when quick lessons can be powerfully provided, *especially* during times of good behavior. Catching kids in their good moments takes a bit of conscious effort, but it is worthwhile. Providing a few quick words of encouragement is powerful in promoting good behavior. They'll appreciate that you noticed and will remember that feeling for a long time!

Scheduling

- Most homes do well with maintaining a regular schedule. Still, it is important to recognize *why* we do it. It is not just for convenience, although it really does help the system run smoothly, but it also affects the process of attachment. Providing a consistent pattern in the day, when the child has expectations of certain things happening predictably, reduces anxiety and allows the development of trust, a major component necessary for healthy attachment.

- Proper scheduling requires energy and dedication. Once again, energy applied to the situation organizes the system and reduces chaos. Chaos sucks up energy, producing more chaos, and eventually results in a breakdown of the system.
- Consistent bedtimes, mealtimes, and awakening times assist in keeping the system running smoothly. There are always exceptions to the rules, but maintain a normal standard for most days, with the exception of special occasions.
- Following a schedule changes the way the brain works, improving growth, mood stability, and sleep patterns.
- Maintaining a structured schedule is a major issue for assisting the child to get back on a normal developmental pattern.

For some facilities, having a written schedule of activities can be helpful especially for the new ones and can serve to remind the caregivers that they may need to get back on track. Having the security of events occurring in a generally predictable pattern serves to provide a good measure of security.

Rituals

- **Rituals produce a sense of community and belonging**. Portions of cultural and personal identity are tied to rituals. Having regularly observed events helps to develop and maintain important parts of the identity. This also provides an opportunity to do important things together as a family.
- **It is very important to put forth the energy to develop and maintain appropriate rituals**. Energy is needed to remember to make the events important and meaningful. Be creative so as to make it interesting. Make sure you understand what the ritual means and how important it is to perpetuate.
- **Cultural rituals help maintain a sense of identity**. These practices celebrate belonging to a particular culture, providing an important sense of identity and history. Some cultural rituals include what we do as Christians, the main identity we wish to instill in our children.
- **Daily rituals include prayer before meals, devotion time before bed or in the morning, and how we greet one another throughout the day.** As we sit down to a meal, rather than chaotically diving into the provided food, attention is requested. Everyone assumes a prayer stance, whether holding hands, folding hands, or bowing the head to show reverence to God. All are quiet while one addresses our Lord in a respectful manner. This reminds us all that every good

gift comes from God—all our provisions, food, money, shelter, everything is from Him, and to Him, we owe gratitude.

Mealtime prayer and devotion assist with putting God in His place, on His throne, in charge of the universe, the one who keeps us and provides for us. That is part of the hierarchy very much needed in the Christian home. As we end the day, we may gather for prayer or we may start the day with Bible reading and prayer. At devotion time, there needs to be some flexibility so that spiritual questions can be addressed briefly together as a group and maybe offer time individually to those having some struggles in any area.

Proper greetings help maintain the adult-child hierarchy. In American culture, we do not hold so much to the greeting as in nearly every other culture, but it remains important in America as well. Prior to addressing adult staff, the children need to learn to extend a respectful "good morning," "good afternoon," or "good evening." In Asian cultures, there might be a bow, in other cultures a handshake. The children learn what is appropriate to their culture, and this helps establish proper boundaries and respect. Part of the ritual is also to learn to not interrupt unless it is an urgent matter. Maintaining rituals emphasizes the hierarchy and promotes proper boundaries and respect for one another.

Special Rituals

- Birthdays: This is a special time for each child. Sometimes, we do not know a child's birthdate for some time after his or her arrival. Once it is obtained, it needs to be a special day. In the case of large homes, allocate a special day for all those celebrating birthdays during the month. The celebration can be within cultural norms, but it needs to have the blessing provided by one of the staff in the form of a special prayer for the child's upcoming year. Be as creative as you can with this.
- Anniversaries: Recognize special days with special meanings, maybe a wedding anniversary of a staff member or the remembrance of the founding of that particular home. This makes a good excuse for a bit of cake or other treat and a special prayer of blessing.
- Christmas: Most of the world's Christians in some way celebrate the birth of our Savior. The type of celebration might vary substantially from place to place, but it is a special day. How one celebrates mostly depends on the culture in that location and perhaps some family rituals that are incorporated. There might be gift-giving or some special treats for everyone. The main event, however, needs to

be the reading of the Christmas story in Luke (Luke 2:1–20) and lively discussion about the amazing thing God did by sending His son to save us. Developing some sort of ritual for the occasion is very meaningful and impactful to children.

- Resurrection Sunday: Though many Christians celebrate the resurrection each Sunday, memorializing it with the Lord's Supper, many areas celebrate a special day during the year to recognize His resurrection. There might be some cultural differences, but it is important to incorporate the story of the resurrection along with some time to reflect on this and remember the great sacrifice that was made on our behalf and the overcoming of death with the victory of His resurrection. It is a joyous occasion and needs to be celebrated as such. It is essential also that we avoid the associated pagan rituals for what in many cultures was a converted pagan holiday.
- National Holidays: God has made it clear that we should "honor the king," meaning that we respect our country and its leaders, obey the laws, and share in the special celebrations. This provides us a sense of belonging to our country and culture. Enjoy the day with culturally appropriate activities, along with some history lesson by way of a story that defines the reason for the celebration. And as always, enjoy a wonderful opportunity to worship God, the almighty and true King.
- Special Cultural Days: Some cultures have other special days of observation. We need to be careful what these are about. Some are very pagan and involve a type of reverence to false gods. We need to teach the children about these but not to involve ourselves in the celebrations. The staff must be familiar with the culture and what the various celebrations really mean. This can be a time of teaching about the history of the culture and can be developed into a positive experience.

Rite-of-Passage Rituals

It is especially important to mark special "rite of passage" events, which signal going from one stage of life to another. Each major step in life as we develop needs to be marked so that we have the idea etched in our mind that we have shifted from one set of circumstances to the next stage. "I was…now I am…" With a new stage, new responsibilities are present, and rites of passage signify readiness to face those:

- ***Graduation from kindergarten, primary school, high school, or college.*** Marking the accomplishment not only serves to improve the self-esteem and self-image, but also readies the child for the next important stage. She or he is passing on to a new stage of life with new challenges.

- ***Preteen to teen birthdays, a special time to discuss sexuality and development.*** This might be around the twelfth or thirteenth birthday. Some homes provide a special retreat for those reaching that stage, at which time they can be instructed in sexuality, what is right and wrong, and how to resist the temptation to adopt others' lack of morality. This can be combined with special activities, athletic competitions, or other activities to make it special. (See chapter 12: Sexuality Education in the Home.)
- ***Blessings—special prayers and affirmations at special times.*** When the child is celebrating something special, it is very important to ask God's blessing on his or her life and future direction. This helps us all to see how important God is in our lives and futures and to continue to lean on Him for the help and guidance we need. (Consider reading *The Blessing: Giving the Gift of Unconditional Love and Acceptance* by John Trent and Gary Smalley.)
- ***Photography.*** Another way to assist in the sense of belonging in the home is the use of photographs and albums to memorialize prior events and stages in life. Pictures can be displayed in the home and changed as new things happen and other children join the home. When a child departs, he or she might wish to have some photos, perhaps in the form of an album, to take along for reminiscing about the events of childhood.

Boundaries

- **Interpersonal Space**: This is often culturally defined but generally gauged according to our own comfort levels. We need to maintain proper space and only invade someone's personal space when given permission to do so. This is like an invisible bubble around us. You can be close, but not too close. You can touch the shoulder or arm, but other areas are out of bounds as a general rule.
- **Greetings**: This helps us to maintain proper social distance. Some children will tolerate a hug as part of the greeting; others will not. For some, a hug or other physical contact is sexually arousing so is to be avoided. (See chapter 11: Sexual Abuse and Sexualized Children.) Greetings, as mentioned previously, also help keep the hierarchy in place.
- **Respect for Property**: We must maintain respect for the children's property and also teach them respect for others' property. Room searches are only done

when indicated. There must be a reason, such as suspected drugs, contraband, thoughts of self-harm, harm to others, or suspicion of food hoarding (rotting food can get rather nasty). There might be situations in which increased vigilance is necessary to keep the child from harm.

- **Touching**: Guidelines regarding touching must be put in place in every facility. In a private home, there must also be guidelines developed so as to maintain good boundaries. Appropriate hugs and physical touch or the shoulder, arm, or back are OK except when a child is not able to tolerate it. It is important that touch is provided only with a child's permission. Eye contact is not forced but invited. If it is not tolerated, it is not pursued. As the relationship progresses, the eye contact will also progress.
- **Language**: Verbal language must be proper and not wander into vulgarities or inappropriate areas such as sexuality, unless specific questions are being asked, which are best addressed by a same-sex houseparent. Inappropriate language must be noted and corrected. Generally, verbal correction is adequate. Most of the children coming from the street life have quite the vulgar vocabulary and have to gradually adapt as they learn what is considered proper.
- **Appropriate Sexuality**: Maintaining appropriate boundaries between staff and children, as well as between the children, is vitally important. Many learned their behaviors from the street culture and do not understand what is right and wrong. Appropriate touching and teaching about privacy and respecting one's own body can help and must be a part of the general teaching in the home. Remember to keep an eye on activities between same-sex children, as well as between boys and girls.
- **Privacy**: This is about the child's personal space, as well as an understanding about modesty and personal possessions. Staffers should not invade a child's privacy unless warranted, as noted above.

Hierarchy

- Parents/caregivers are in charge; children are not.
- All battles must be won by staff, so choose wisely. (Remember, love *always* wins.)
- Caregivers in group homes need to be clearly aware of lines of authority.
- Energy is needed to maintain the system's integrity. When it is lacking, children take power.

When there are clear lines of authority, the system is much more secure. Each individual needs to know his or her role. The children are children; adults are in charge. When battles must be engaged, it is important that we are careful to make sure that it is fair and that the outcome does not place the child in charge. It does not change the hierarchy for you to admit an honest mistake and seek forgiveness of the child, but it serves to strengthen the relationship and maintain the hierarchy. There also needs to be room for dialogue to discuss the why and wherefore of decisions that are made. To maintain the hierarchy, the director of the home must continually be strong and effective as a leader. Jesus taught us the concept of servant leadership—this is how leadership works in the orphanage.

Roles and Responsibilities

- Each member of a system has a defined role and responsibilities that accompany that role.
- The role of being a child is to play, learn, grow, and interact appropriately with others.
- As children are able, more work-related tasks are assigned to teach more responsibility.
- Parents/caregivers other personnel have special roles, as assigned by management, to fulfill responsibilities as parental figures, teachers, or other roles.

Conclusion

Providing positive energy to the system involves fulfilling one's role, communicating well with other team members, other members of the family, confirming boundaries, providing positive affirmation (energy) to coworkers, and doing your part to maintain structural integrity.

Positive energy invested in the system produces system integrity (wholeness), which then allows the structure to persist so that its purpose is maintained.

Negative energy destroys the system's integrity, produces chaos, and alters the system's purpose, making the system run poorly and not produce the results desired.

The purpose of the system is to produce ***productive, committed Christian adults.***

Notes

3

Normal Development and Attachment

To effectively negotiate a child's successful arrival to adulthood and to offer the best chance of that child becoming a productive member of society, it is vital that the process of attachment be completed in a way that allows the development of healthy, strong relationships. The process takes most of the growing-up years but starts early. With each new experience of the infant, more layers of complexity are created in the brain—more connections and richer connections, to allow more complex. If not completed successfully, the child's adjustment to adult life can be very difficult.

The process starts at the very beginning of life, in the mother's womb:

- *In utero*, once hearing is developed, the sounds of mother and father are likely heard and will be recognized after birth.
- *At birth*, the infant takes in the smell, voice, and touch of its caregiver and preferentially will seek out its mother's voice, sometimes even the father if he was involved during the pregnancy.

- *After birth*, the next phase of attachment begins.

Basic Needs, Basic States

The developing infant starts out with six states:

1. Awake Alert
2. Awake Crying
3. Awake Somnolent
4. Light Sleep
5. Dream Sleep
6. Deep Sleep

Attachment is based on consistently meeting the basic needs of the infant in all its states without causing the infant to become overly frustrated

- **Awake alert:** In this state, the infant is looking for input—emotional, physical, visual, tactile, auditory—taking in incredible bits of information that are processed into later development of language and emotion. Even shortly after birth, there is an effort to imitate caregiver movements and expressions. At this stage, we must provide input and interaction, particularly talking and visual stimuli. Neglect inhibits brain growth and development.
- **Awake crying:** The child is expressing a need. The caregiver assesses in a timely manner what is the matter and responds—maybe a change of diaper, some food, a warm blanket, genuine affection, or loving attention. Response in a timely manner develops trust. Neglect fosters distrust and a sense of futility, which can lead to a depressive state.
- **Awake somnolent:** The child might be waking or going to sleep. The need is for a quiet, safe, secure environment of the proper temperature. Upon the child's awakening, instill quietness and maybe hold him or her to allow a gradual return to the wakeful state. Meeting the child's physical needs prior to sleep onset and after waking builds trust and consistency, allowing the child to see the world as a nice place.
- **Light sleep:** The need is for a quiet, comfortable location so sleep can be consummated or a wakeful state can be gradually assumed.

- **Dream sleep:** If the day was chaotic, full of yelling and conflict, the dream state reflects this with disrupted sleep patterns. Enjoying a peaceful home situation promotes nice dreams and reduces anxiety, allowing trust to develop.
- **Deep sleep:** A quiet safe environment is needed. This is when growth occurs. If chaos reigns in the home and this sleep state cannot be adequately maintained for a necessary number of hours, there can be physical consequences with growth and developmental delays.

As the above states are addressed adequately, the child starts out feeling quite secure and loved. This forms the foundation on which the development can build upon and attachment can proceed. Now we will look at what happens over the next several months and years. The need states will change and become a bit more complicated with age but the principle remains of meeting the various need states in a timely fashion with a minimum of frustration.

- **During the first few months,** integration occurs—taking in, processing, and sorting the sights and sounds of those closely associated.
- **At around eight months**, some stranger anxiety develops, attachment matures, and the child prefers to be with those people who have participated most consistently and effectively with the child rather than with strangers who are not closely associated with him or her. This is usually the mother or father but can be an older sibling as well. This is a major step, a developmental milestone when the attachment process really begins, which then allows specific and preferential trust to develop.
- **From eight to around eighteen months**, maturing of attachment occurs. This grows to the point of separation, which is another major milestone. The baby ventures out into the world, where he or she can tolerate being separated for a time from the person with whom they have a primary attachment. This is, however, marked by some insecurity and separation anxiety. The child will separate physically from the mother, go play in another room, and then return to refuel, to check to see if mother is still there. This being consistent, the child can proceed with becoming a person on his own, which is called *psychological birth.*
- **From eighteen months to three years**, individuation matures to the point of tolerating longer periods of separation. During this time, the child internalizes a picture of the primary attachment—mother, older sibling, or the caregiver—and is able to develop an internal *holding* environment. There is a deeply held

internalized image of, usually, the mother. This is conjured up in the mind when self-calming is needed and serves to assist with regulation of emotions, anxiety, and distress. In a sense, the child can *hold* himself, now more able to self-calm under minor stress, but that might not be quite enough. The image of mother might be hard to bring up, so a transitional object might help with this. It could be a stuffed animal, blanket, or special toy. This object will stay with the child for months or even a year or so, as a representation of the object of attachment. It disappears when no longer needed.

- **From three to five years**, the child begins to explore more of the world and interact with peers, learning parallel and interactive play. There are now distancing and approximating behaviors, testing the strength of the attachment bond. The child behaves in such a way as to distance himself from the attachment object in order to observe the reaction. These are behaviors designed to move the parent away from the child. Is there rejection or correction and love? There are also behaviors designed to endear you to the child. Do they work? Was anyone paying attention? Parental reaction to these important behaviors shapes attachment, whether it becomes secure or insecure.
- **From five to eight years**, peer relationships develop with the same sequence of strong attachment, then separation-individuation to healthy relationship. The pattern continues through life. With a basis of positive relationships with primary caregivers, the child can continue moral development, rules for right and wrong, playing games with rules, structured interactions with peers via school, and sports activities. If the foundation is not properly laid, moral development can lag.
- **From eight to eleven years**, individuation proceeds with further development of an accurate sense of self and identity within a structure of family and culture. "Who am I? Where did I come from?"

As the child's development progresses, the need states become much more complex. However, the basic premise remains:

- **From ages 12 to 14** starts the reworking of the initial attachment. There is approximation (coming close) with primary object of attachment, usually mother, spending more time, more talking more, having more usually positive interaction, but only for a few months or so, then some distancing approximating behaviors culminating in further individuation. This would include behaviors of asserting independence, being resistive, testing boundaries and exploring more of the outside world. The reworking of attachment can be corrective if the initial attachment did not go so well. At this time also peer group identification increases as the individuation progresses. There is a desire to be independent and different but just like everyone in their peer group. There is interest in, and unstable attachments to opposite sex. Further self-image development as secondary sexual development and hormonal changes occur. This brings about a good deal of confusion at times if there is difficulty identifying what is the proper gender role for the individual and accepting who you are.

- **From ages 15 to 17** There is further separation and individuation from parents. There occur some cultural rites of passage activities such as driver's license, dating permission, job acquisition and other events dependent on the culture. There is a more stable connection to opposite sex, relationships are more enduring but still can be quite unstable.
- **From 18 to 21** Independence preparation proceeds which starts with some of the rites of passage and continues with development of career interests, self-image clarification, possible choice of life partner, and initiation of adult responsibilities.

Success with independence as a young adult depends heavily on the building blocks of development and attachment.

Attachment is based on consistently meeting the basic needs of the child in all his/her states without causing the child to become overly frustrated.

Normal Development and Attachment Quick Reference

- **During first months of life**, there is integration of the sights and sounds of those closely associated.
- **At around eight months**, there is some stranger anxiety, attachment matures, and child prefers objects of attachment.
- **At eight to eighteen months**, expect maturing of attachment to the point of separation causing psychological birth, marked by some insecurity and separation anxiety, will separate physically from mother figure and then return to refuel.
- **At eighteen months to three years**, individuation matures to the point of tolerating longer periods of separation, as the child internalizes a picture of the object of attachment and an internal holding environment, now more able to self-calm under minor stress, and might use a transitional object.
- **At three years to five years**, child begins to explore more of the world, starts to interact with peers, learns parallel and interactive play, and might exhibit distancing approximating behaviors.
- **At five years to eight years**, peer relationships develop with same sequence of strong attachment followed by separation individuation to healthy relationship. With basis of positive relationship with primary caregivers, child can now continue moral development, rules for right and wrong, play games with rules, structured interactions with peers via school, and sport activities.
- **At eight years to eleven years**, individuation proceeds with further development of an accurate sense of self and identity within the structure of family and culture. Peer relations tend toward group relations but still with special relationships generally of the same sex.
- **Twelve years to fourteen years** heralds the reworking of the initial attachment, approximation with primary object of attachment, usually mother, spending more time, more talking, more interaction, but only for a few months or so, then some distancing and approximating behaviors culminating in further individuation.
- **At fourteen years to seventeen years**, expect further separation and individuation from parents. Cultural rite-of-passage activities occur, such as driver's license, dating permission, and job acquisition. More stable connection to the opposite sex develops, and relationships are more enduring but still can be quite unstable.
- **Eighteen years to twenty-one years** marks independence preparation, which starts with some of the rites of passage and continues with development of career interests, self-image, possible choice of life partner, and initiation of adult responsibilities. Success with independence is dependent on the building blocks of attachment and development.

Notes

Reactive Attachment Disorder

When things go wrong, attachment does not occur like it is supposed to in normal development. Then, there is a characteristic set of symptoms, commonly known as Attachment Disorder or Reactive Attachment Disorder (RAD). The diagnostic criteria as per the American Psychiatric Association's *Diagnostic and Statistical Manual of Mental Disorders*, fifth edition (*DSM-5*) reads as follows:

Reactive Attachment Disorder 313.89 (F94.1)

A. A consistent pattern of inhibited, emotionally withdrawn behavior toward adult caregivers, manifested by both of the following:
   1. The child rarely or minimally seeks comfort when distressed
   2. The child rarely or minimally responds to comfort offered when distressed

B. A persistent social and emotional disturbance characterized by at least two of the following:
    1. Minimal social and emotional responsiveness to others
    2. Limited positive affect
    3. Episodes of unexplained irritability, sadness, or fearfulness which are evident during nonthreatening interactions with adult caregivers

C. The child has experienced a pattern of extremes of insufficient care as evidenced by at least one of the following:

    1. Social neglect or deprivation in the form of persistent lack of having basic emotional needs for comfort, stimulation, and affection met by caregiving adults.
    2. Repeated changes in primary caregivers that limit opportunities to form stable attachments (e.g., frequent changes in foster care)
    3. Rearing in unusual settings that severely limit opportunities to form selective attachments (e.g., institutions with high child to caregiver ratios).

D. Does not meet the criteria for Autism Spectrum Disorder
E. Disturbance is evident before age five
F. Child has a developmental age of at least nine months.
Specify current severity: Reactive attachment disorder is specified as severe when a child exhibits all symptoms of the disorder, with each symptom manifesting at relatively high levels. Reprinted with permission from the Diagnostic and Statistical Manual of Mental Disorders, 5th Ed. (Copyright ©2013). American Psychiatric Association. All rights reserved.

When Things Go Wrong

Many things can cause a disruption of attachment. The child might suffer from the disorder never having been away from his natural parents. More often, however, the child has suffered removal from the natural home for any of a variety of reasons. The severity of the disorder depends on many factors.

Attachment can be disrupted by any of the following:

- **Emotionally distant parents:** Some parents are too busy to connect to their child. They might not spend much time talking to the child or interacting in a way that promotes attachment. Due to parents being unavailable, the child might have a primary attachment to another relative or someone at the day care. This sometimes does not work out well.
- **Physical abuse:** This produces a violation of trust. The child does not know how the parent is going to react in any given situation. If there is a great deal of anger in the family system, this further disrupts a safe attachment.
- **Sexual abuse:** This is highly dependent on the level of abuse but has two effects: (1) betrayal of trust and (2) premature sexualization, which contaminates the parent-child relation. True love and concern are often absent where sexual abuse is present, and in their place is intense pain, or even pleasure, that is truly confusing to the developing child. Being able to trust and attach is very difficult in this situation.
- **Inconsistent caregivers:** This can result from multiple placements in different homes or families (such as foster care in some countries). Each time a child is moved, there is less chance of making a good attachment with the subsequent placement. Caregiving might be inconsistent even within a family due to stress, economic problems, a mother with successive partners, or a father who is only intermittently involved.
- **Placement outside of the natural family:** Any child placed in a children's home, foster home, or adoptive home, or one who is living on the street is vulnerable to the disorder as he or she likely did not have the chance to begin or continue the process of attachment.
- **Neglect:** This is probably one of the strongest predictors of the disorder. Early neglect can actually prove fatal if not remedied. Without the first stages of bonding, a child develops no will to live. Subsequent neglect provides emotional starvation and lack of trust, but a child with that difficulty *can* attach in a supportive, structured, corrective environment.

Attachment disorder can occur not just in abandoned street kids but also in some unexpected situations. While in my child psychiatry training, my first wife, Ellen, was a preschool teacher. She was working in a church day care located in a very elite upper-class neighborhood. After work one day, she engaged in a conversation about what could be the matter with the children who seemingly had everything yet were so difficult to manage in the preschool. I suggested we do a bit of detective work on our own. She was instructed in how to administer a projective test used for that age of child, which consists of drawing a house, tree, and person. She brought them back to me for scoring. It was shocking what the pictures revealed. Over half of the children had findings in the drawings indicative of a serious attachment problem as well as some issues with self-image. I inquired further as to how the interaction seemed between the child and the parent coming to collect them from the preschool. One typical scenario was the mother coming in for the child and not really greeting the child but taking her hand. On the way out, she stops to talk with the director of the school, chatting about where she and her husband would be going next, what vacations and trips they had planned, and where they would eat that night. Meanwhile, little Sally is pulling on her mother's arm, attempting to get her attention. "Mommy, Mommy, look what I made for you." She attempts in vain to get her mother's attention. Soon, they go out the door. As Ellen departs from the church, she notices some of the hard work of the children blowing about in the parking lot. It made us both very sad. We decided to try an intervention. The director was very much in favor and cooperated very well. When the next afternoon came around and the first mother was at the door talking to the director, she requested that the mother get down close and talk to her child and respond to what she was saying. Most parents were a bit taken aback but did comply and found the conversation a bit awkward at first. Gradually, behaviors improved, and there was more talk from the children about their parents rather than the nannies or sitters. The real culmination came one day when we were in a fast-food restaurant with a play area. As we were finishing giving our order, a young mother came running up to Ellen and gave her a big hug. She apparently found out who had been responsible for the intervention. This millionaire wife and mother was in the play area having a blast with her five-year-old daughter, enjoying being a mother and connecting with her child.

Developmental Vulnerability

During various stages of development, there are special times when the child, or even the adult, is more vulnerable to the effects of trauma than at other times. Trauma can be defined as simply as a separation from the primary attachment, usually the mother, or more serious situations noted above.

Early Disruption

- **At birth.** A baby removed from its mother at birth can suffer short-term irritability and depression but is generally able to recover well. While the baby has a good ability to recover from this, many an adult who did not know his or her birth mother try very hard to find her. This shows that the connection can be very strong, even at birth.
- **Birth to seven months.** Disruption can result in failure to thrive, depression, inhibited brain development, and delayed attachment so severe that the child might become gravely or mortally ill just from not being attended to emotionally.
- **Seven to nine months.** This is a time of developmental vulnerability. Disruption can result in marked delays in attachment and social development, poor modulation of emotions, irritability, anger, and lack of self-control.
- **Nine to seventeen months.** Disruption is generally better tolerated if attachment with caregiver was attained, providing some resiliency and ability to attach to the next caregiver. Disruption that does not include a good bit of trauma is generally manageable.
- **Eighteen months to three years.** Again, this is a more vulnerable period. If disruption occurs, this delays separation-individuation, development of self, and internalization of maternal object. If not resolved and was due to trauma, it can result in borderline personality and often produces classical RAD (reactive attachment disorder) symptoms.
- **Three to six years.** If the parent-child relationship was stable prior to disruption at this age, recovery is good if placement is consistent or the child can be returned home. If there are prior problems, the child might continue to have RAD symptoms, as well as impairment of personality development and social relatedness, particularly delayed moral development.
- **Six to twelve years.** Response is dependent on the child's resilience and prior trauma. If the first six years have gone well, trauma was minimal, and attachment was secure, then during this phase, there is relatively less risk, and the child will likely be able to recover well and return to normal development. If the child has already been damaged by a traumatic early life, there may be problems, especially with peer relations.
- **Twelve to eighteen years.** Adolescent rapprochement, the reworking of the attachment, is important to the final steps of attachment. If not able to complete this step, the child will lack skills in relating to the opposite sex. She or he will

also demonstrate impairment of self-regulation and have poor development of self-esteem.

Treatment

- **External structure.** Supportive care, consequences to behavior, regular scheduling, meeting of needs in a timely manner, managing crises, and so forth lead to internal structure as the attachment progresses. This is brain tract development.
- **Proper treatment in the home.** Occasionally, medication is helpful to address some very disturbing symptoms. In some areas, medications are not available so the home is the only treating environment.
- **A consistently supportive environment.** This is why *structure* is vital. It allows the security for the attachment to start taking place.
- **Caregiver response to needs.** As with the infant, provide what is needed on a consistent basis, offering the reassurance that needs will be met. "You don't have to worry about your next meal here."
- **Trusting relationships.** As you are consistent with the child, trust can develop. This is the basis of the attachment.
- **Redefining behaviors.** Approach and avoidance (distancing, approximating) can be helpful in controlling the reaction of the caregiver. As you analyze behaviors, look for indications that the child is trying to distance from you or draw you in closer since both types of behaviors occur. The child is asking, "Can I trust you? Will you throw me out if I am this bad? If I am good, will you like me better?" You can then more appropriately answer the question the child does not know he or she is asking.
- **Response to the need states.** Answer the question the behavior is asking. Mainly, the question is whether or not it is safe to attach to caregivers in this environment, and the answer has to be one of encouragement. "You are safe here, and we love you."
- **Assistance with crisis states.** States of crisis generally occur about every three months with attachment disorders. Weathering the serious crises, understanding they are coming from distress in the child trying to decide whether or not to attach, can make a big difference in his or her life.
- **Assistance in defining feeling states.** Sources of emotion include the developmental anger from frustrated attachment. Help the child define *all* the feelings he or she is experiencing, not just anger.

- **Use of restraint procedures.** Holding a child who is overwhelmed by anger and not able to control himself, when done properly, can help to assist with attachment. (See comments in this chapter on Discipline.)
- **Use of appropriate physical contact.** Hugs, physical touching when tolerated, and gradually increasing eye contact duration all serve to further attachment.
- **Use of hand cream to permit touch.** For toddlers and even the older child, the use of hand cream, associated with words of acceptance and encouragement, could be helpful with touch-sensitive girls—boys might not like the cream.

While visiting a children's home in Baja, California, I spent time observing in the toddler's house. There were perhaps twenty toddlers in the main playroom with one caregiver.

Each child was focused on his or her toy or activity. The caregiver picked up a hand lotion container and snapped it open. All the children went on alert and turned their attention in response to that sound. They hurried to the caregiver who, taking each child, applied some hand cream and provided words of encouragement and love. After the process, the room was alive with chatter. The children were able to get some needed fuel. The need for emotional input and connection is so important that the child craves attention like one would crave food after a long fast.

- Use one-on-one time as a human-interaction reward for appropriate behaviors rather than always using material rewards. This can assist in promoting the relationship. It is very important that the opposite—the withdrawing of love—never be used as a negative consequence.
- Assist the child with tolerating normal touch, hugs, and eye contact without forcing it on him or her.
- Older children can be educated regarding RAD (reactive attachment disorder) and what they need to do to help attachment progress.
- The process of corrective attachment takes about three years to complete if the child is not resistant.
- In the case of multiple placement failures, a longer time is required.

Pharmacology Targeting Specific Behaviors

Medications are generally a short-term help while attachment proceeds. Unless there is an underlying mental disorder, the medications generally can be discontinued over time. Some locations do not have many of the following medication groups, but doctors in your area might have other medications that are close:

- **Anxiety:** SSRI preferred, such as Fluoxetine and Citalopram, or benzodiazepines sometimes in older children
- **Rage:** carbamazepine, divalproex, valproic acid, atypicals such as risperdone
- **Impulsive/compulsive behaviors:** SSRIs, atypicals, or if hyperactive possibly stimulants
- **Hyperactivity:** Stimulants, including methylphenidate or amphetamine salts, especially for those who are too hyperactive to pay sufficient attention to begin the attachment process

Behavioral measures with consistent application of appropriate consequences are essential.

- The child must be taught boundaries, as these did not develop naturally.
- The child must be assisted with self-regulation until system develops over time to self-regulate.

Consequences of Success

If corrective attachment proceeds well, the child can grow up to be a healthy functional adult.

Completed attachment may lead to:

- A good moral framework
- Adequate interpersonal boundaries
- Normal understanding of emotions and good control of them
- Adequate control of anger
- Ability to see the perspective of others, understand the distress of others, and respond to needs of others
- Less narcissism and a more caring attitude
- Reciprocity in relationships and a good sense of give-and-take
- A good understanding of the concept of love
- Adequate sense of self
- Ability to have loyalty toward others
- Decreased probability of substance abuse
- Less probability of ending up in a criminal lifestyle

Reflecting on the above, one can see that the opposite would hold true with those who were not able to successfully complete the attachment process.

Special Issues

In the process of development, a child from a family of multiple siblings might have a primary attachment to an older sibling. This is almost always the case, even in normal families with sibling groups of more than four children. If the child's parents are not doing their job, an older child will step into the role. In that case, even with fewer than four siblings, the attachment can be with an older sibling. This is important in the consideration of placement. If you cannot fit all five or more siblings in one home, it is best to place the younger one or two with an older one, so as to preserve the attachment.

This phenomenon can also come into play when the children are not making progress with attachment in a placement home. An older sibling might not have provided implicit permission for a younger child to make attachments to the caregiver or to share certain family secrets or trauma that could interfere with subsequent development. To facilitate attachment when this occurs, it is necessary to gain trust with the older sibling (or the one holding the power in the sibling group) and gradually promote the idea that it is OK for them to stay in the home and to connect with the caregivers. Sometimes, a well-informed counselor can assist with this process.

Notes

5

Basics of Behavior Management

A very common reason for placement in the home to not work out well is the emergence of behaviors that go beyond the caregiver's ability to manage. With the basic understanding of behaviors and some tools to deal with the challenges that will inevitably appear, success becomes much more likely, and your stress level will be much less.

The other important aspect of managing behaviors is the concept of promoting the good behaviors. In so doing, many of the negatives become less intense. As we demonstrate positive values ourselves, the children will start to pick up on it. If we create interventions that incorporate the values we want to impart, that also serves to help mold them into the people God wants them to be.

Understanding the reason for the behaviors is very important. If we can see beyond the behavior to the child and not define the child by the behavior, we can instead for-give the behaviors once consequence is applied and start anew thereafter.

> Children, obey your parents in the Lord, for this is right. "Honor your father and mother"—which is the first commandment with a promise—"so that it may go well with you and that you may enjoy long life on the earth."
> Fathers, do not exasperate your children; instead, bring them up in the training and instruction of the Lord.
>
> —Ephesians 6:1–4

Understanding Behavior

- *All behavior has a purpose.*
- *It is usually trying to communicate something, test something, or provoke something.*
- *It might be the product of or contributed to by a mental illness or developmental disorder.*
- *Our response to behavior serves to increase it, decrease it, or extinguish it altogether.*
- *Our own attitudes and reactions to the child might unknowingly promote very negative behaviors.*
- *We must always be aware of what we are doing, communicating, promoting, or extinguishing.*

As we try to come to terms with understanding behavior, we need to have the basic concept of what it is and how to manage it in a way so that we are doing the best for the *child.* The goals of behavior management are to teach the child what is proper and normal, help him or her attain the behaviors appropriate to his or her developmental stage, assist with acquiring morality and basic rules for life, and ultimately produce productive Christian adults. Not all behavior is bad. It is merely what we do in a particular circumstance. We want to promote the good and extinguish or lessen the bad so that a good moral framework is developed. We also need to take care not to allow the behavior to define who the child is but to unconditionally love the child apart from the behaviors. This requires us to exercise the forgiveness we are capable of as followers of Christ.

We influence behaviors generally through reinforcement, applying some type of consequence that either promotes or discourages a particular behavior. These come in three varieties:

1. negative reinforcement, that which serves to ***not*** reinforce the behavior;
2. positive reinforcement, that which serves to promote desired behaviors; and
3. unintentional reinforcement, that which we do unintentionally, which may serve to reinforce or discouraged desired or undesired behaviors.

Behaviors can also be extinguished if ignored, that is, paying no attention to them. However, this must be used judiciously as certain behaviors may escalate to a level that has to have some consequence applied.

Negative Reinforcement

Do not let the word *negative* give you the idea that this is something negative or bad. This just means that we are ***not*** reinforcing the behavior. Some types of negative reinforcement would be considered abusive or designed to cause harm rather than maintain the goal of teaching what is proper and good and to maintain love and acceptance for the child. Most is quite appropriate and helpful. Positive reinforcement promotes the behavior. The use of negative reinforcement, though necessary, needs to be done with love and a bit of flexibility so as to not overwhelm children with the consequences. Until they arrived in your facility or home, their lives were probably already very negative, with very little positive going on. The approaches are to help teach each child what not to do.

- **Discipline:** Negative consequences designed to teach, discipline might include some discomfort and loss of freedom, but has an aspect of providing information that promotes appropriate behavior.
- **Natural consequences:** An example is a child told not to run on the loose gravel as she will get hurt, but she does and so gets hurt. Sometimes this, plus some words to associate the natural consequence with the behavior, might be sufficient to provide the necessary lesson.
- **Verbal correction:** Properly applied, verbal correction can provide a good impact. Words that are too harsh, long-winded, or delivered from loss of control by the corrector might have the opposite impact, promoting the undesired behavior.
- **Withdrawal of affect (emotion, positive regard, love):** This occurs when the child receives the message that, due to behavior, the caregiver no longer cares for the child—he or she is no longer loved or desired. Especially with a poorly attached child, this strengthens his belief that no one cares for him. It is a negative consequence that does not have a positive outcome. We must avoid expressing anything that the child might interpret as an indication that our love is conditional.
- **Punishment:** Generally, not designed to teach, punishment might consist of inflicting physical pain or confining someone for a period of time, such as in

jail or detention. This approach is more when a tough love approach is needed and nothing else is working. It must still be done in love and not in anger.

- **Time-out:** This really means time out from attention. It can be very effective if properly applied for the defined behaviors.

Time-Out Procedure

- Define a few behaviors to work with, such as defiance, talking back, disobedience, fighting, and so forth.
- Find a boring corner and a chair for the child to sit during time-out, and try to use this spot consistently if possible.
- Explain the process to the child. This is best done when not responding to a behavior. "This is what we are going to do when you [define the unwanted behaviors], and this is how we will do it."
- Use the same process each time.
- When behavior occurs, you say, "You have done what we've asked you not to do, and so you are going to time-out." No other words are spoken. Ignore the protestations; do not respond to them.
- If the child will not go willingly, help him to the chair. If he refuses to go, other consequences might be needed.
- Use one minute per year of age. For example, a three-year-old sits for three minutes. Time-out is not usually helpful for those over ten years of age.
- Using some type of timing device—kitchen timer, watch, or stopwatch— start the time when the child is sitting quietly. If the protests begin or the child says something, just restart the clock without saying a word. The time is complete if the child sits quietly for the designated time.
- At the end of the prescribed time, the child is released. If there is no damage to clean up, then give just a word or two about improving his behavior and let him go. No lengthy discussions are needed since he already has completed the consequence.

Restraint

This is reserved for serious disruptive or violent behavior, when the child is out of control. With the younger children, when properly applied, restraint can assist with lessening attachment-related rage and a sense of loss of control.

Restraint Procedure

- Use the procedure taught to you—most homes dealing with attachment problems have a procedure accepted by the local government. Foster homes need to check as to what can be done legally according the prevailing laws. Make sure it is followed exactly so as to not be abusive.
- Define the behavior for which this will be employed, generally disruption, disobedience, hitting, kicking, tantrums, and verbal or physical rage.
- Attempt to negotiate prior to the procedure. If there are no results, close your mouth and proceed with the restraint using only words to those helping you with the process.
- Maintain the process until calming occurs.
- Once the child is calm, you can turn him or her to face you, offer some words of encouragement, and ask if he or she wants to talk. If not, the procedure is done. ***Do not overuse words—they will destroy the process.***
- Upon release, the child can then clean up whatever might have been broken.

Grounding

Grounding is a process of removing established privileges that are important to the child so as to mold the identified behavior to be more appropriate.

Grounding Procedure

- Within the structure of the family, there must be privileges that can be earned or lost due to behaviors.
- Grounding implies loss of one or many privileges.
- Decide for what behaviors you would use this with the particular child.
- Find out what privilege seems important to the child.
- Decide on a specific length of time that is reasonable and clearly understood to both parties.
- Included in the grounding might be some ways offered for the child to reduce the time, such as special chores or writing assignments—be creative.
- You might want to avoid telling the child of the grounding reduction and instead provide it as a surprise when assigned tasks are completed and behavior is more appropriate. This turns it into more of a positive experience. The consequence

might be fourteen days of grounding, and at the successful completion of ten days, you might advise the child that she has done well, and if she can continue for one more day, then the grounding is over, or if certain assignments or work is completed, then they are free.

Positive Reinforcement

In order to maintain a healthy environment in the home, it is important to concentrate on the use of positive approaches as much as possible but not to neglect negative reinforcement-related consequences for the times it is necessary to redirect unwanted behaviors. Everything, however, is done in love following the guidelines given us in the Scriptures:

> Fathers do not embitter your children, or they will become discouraged. (Colossians 3:21 NIV)

Basic Guidelines

Positive approaches, when applied properly, are the most potent in promoting behavior change. However, we have to be careful with children who have come from a very negative background—physical abuse, verbal abuse that constantly was putting them down, never being able to please the alcoholic parent, younger children on the street who are low in the hierarchy and whose superiors constantly degrade them. These children are often very sensitive to positive reinforcement. The dose cannot initially be high. Pay attention to the valence or power in your words (see below in Words of Praise section). A child from this background might have finally done something well, so the caregiver uses high-valence words and then later finds the child in her room with everything torn apart crying on her bed. She had an overdose of positive reinforcement and could not handle it.

Another rule with positive reinforcements is the valence or power of the nonverbal reward. We do not want to provide a high-powered reward for just a small positive behavior. We need to carefully consider the value of the reward, as well as the words of praise, so that as with the negative reinforcement, it is appropriate to the level of good behavior.

Positive Reinforcement Approaches

- **Rewards:** For children who are learning to attach, the most powerful rewards are those with a human component. Nonetheless, material rewards are powerful for reinforcing a job well done, appropriate behaviors, or having done something especially good or thoughtful.

- **Special privileges:** Choose a privilege that is out of the ordinary, maybe earned by some special achievement or good schoolwork. This could include such things as staying up a bit later on a non-school night or spending time with friends from outside the facility or home. Creativity is helpful here as well.
- **Words of praise:** Praise for a job well done comes in a variety of strengths or *valence*. If we say, "Good job" or "Job well done," it is positive but of low valence. "Very good" is a bit higher, while "excellent" is higher still. "Fantastic, unbelievable, wow!" is probably the ultimate and is reserved for very special occasions for the older child or the younger child who can tolerate high praise without side effects such as anxiety, becoming overwhelmed, engaging in destructive behaviors, or going into a rage.
- **Monetary allowance:** Within many cultures, the provision of a weekly monetary reward is helpful, at least in learning how to handle money but also in providing the caregiver something to take away if the behavior warrants or to give the child the opportunity to earn more as good behaviors warrant. The amount can be small but enough to buy some inexpensive personal items when going to the store. Some facilities will not be able to afford this, but you could use some other system in which points are earned toward some special time or reward.
- **Special time with parenting figures:** This can be a very powerful reward, especially if the child has had a prior life of rejection. It might be just a trip to the store or ice-cream shop, but it could be as nice as a meal out or a movie, depending on the behavior that is being rewarded.
- **Catching them in good behavior:** This takes a bit of energy but is powerful. During the course of the day, you notice a couple of kids playing well together, sharing, or finally getting along with each other. You can approach them, make brief eye contact, place hands to shoulders of each child, and just say a few words of positive regard: "I really like the way you are playing together today" or "I appreciate that you are getting along." These phrases connect the caregiver to the children in a positive way, as you are expressing appreciation for them. A few carefully planted words of affection can be helpful as well: "We are so happy you came to live in our home" or "We really enjoy having you in our family." We do not want to overdo, but catching a few sincere moments like this is very powerful.

- **Star chart:** This is a system to work with the younger children, ages four through maybe ten or eleven or, if developmentally delayed, maybe older. Make a chart with the days of the week along the top, with the behaviors that need to be promoted or discouraged listed on the side. For each day the goal is met for the behavior, a star is placed. At the earning of a predetermined quantity of stars, an initial reward of low value is given but increases as the stars accumulate. When an unwanted behavior is no longer a problem, it is removed from the list to make room for another problem behavior or some desirable behaviors. (See sample chart.) Charts are easily made on a computer or by hand. Stars can be drawn in or stickers can be used. If possible, the child can place the star in the appropriate column when a task is completed.

	Monday	Tuesday	Wednesday	Thursday	Friday	Saturday	Sunday
Clean Room							
Chores							
Obey							
No Swear Words							

Special Assignments

Special assignments can be positive or negative, but we prefer to keep reinforcements on a positive note. As children grow older and are capable of doing a bit more, sometimes, special work is helpful. This might be used to reduce the time of grounding or as a consequence on its own. It is very important again that the "punishment fit the crime" and to stop and think before reacting so that we respond with reasonable consequences, not based on our anger or frustration. As much as possible, try to make this a positive, even fun, experience of learning together and promoting discussion.

- **Writing assignments:** These are best when related to the behavior in question. One cognitive skill many of the children lack is called *previewing*—that is, being able to see potential consequences of a behavior beforehand. Have an assignment to help the child think about what he or she did. For example, if a child attempted to run away from the home, assign an essay on what would happen if he succeeded in running away, where he would go, what he would, how he would sleep, and what he'd be missing. It can be a short essay, but with the objective of looking at the *what if*. It would then be discussed with the child upon completion so as to assist with this understanding. This can be helpful, but the child must have adequate writing ability.

- **Repetitive writing:** This is commonly used, or overused, in various locations. It might be somewhat helpful with oppositional, hard-to-reach children who need more of a negative approach. The number of sentences must be reasonable and something the child is capable of doing. Repetitive writing of scripture is to be avoided; however, older children might respond to investigating a particular behavior-related theme in the Bible and writing a short report regarding that. Most Bibles have reference sections for looking up specific topics or words if Internet is not available in your location. If a child is forced to write verses over and over, there develops a profound dislike for the scriptures—and this does not fit the goals of the ministry! This is listed under positive reinforcement as it can be promoted to be a positive experience and promote desirable behaviors. It could also be considered a negative reinforcement effectively assisting with stopping unwanted behaviors as well.

Unintentional Reinforcement

Sometimes, without realizing it, we unintentionally reinforce negative or undesired behavior by our reactions. That is why it's important to be aware of how we react to behaviors.

- **Inappropriate reactions of parents:** Perhaps a caregiver does not react to a behavior or reacts with inappropriate humor and does not take it seriously. Some behaviors do not matter, and there is a great deal of healing in laughing with the child. If it is a behavior that goes against the rules of the house, moral standards, politeness, and positive regard for others, we need to react appropriately. Our reaction at that moment is a major determinant of what will happen the next time.
- **Inconsistency with discipline:** Maybe the last time a similar behavior happened, the consequence was lighter or heavier than what is given out this time. Most preteen children, especially the poorly attached, have an overdeveloped sense of justice, so be mindful.
- **Tacit approval:** Something occurs in which we laugh or ignore, but the message is passed along that this behavior is OK with this caregiver.

All humans, even adult caregivers, tend to make mistakes, so it is very important that if we do react in an inappropriate manner to a given behavior that we accept responsibility. We correct our own behavior with an apology to the child and an acknowledgment that we also make mistakes. A humble willing-to-learn attitude goes a long way in being able to continue in a challenging ministry such as this.

Special Considerations

Most of the techniques mentioned above are helpful for the majority of children who come into care. However, there are times when caregivers are unable to figure out what is going on and why. At this point, we need to have a process of thinking that can help us arrive at an answer to help the child. What should we do when the normal approaches are not working, particularly in the following instances?

- Behavior becomes threatening
- Repetitive behaviors that do not respond to the measures in place
- Bizarre and unusual behaviors
- Sudden changes in behavior

In these cases, we need to define and analyze the behaviors so as to design a beneficial approach.

Analyzing Behavior

- **Defining behavior:** Having a vocabulary to describe the behavior is helpful in understanding and communication and also gives us a better idea of what is going on at its core.
- **Type of behavior:** The behavior can be placed in a category to help you understand it.
- **Intensity:** How severe is the behavior?
- **Frequency:** How often does the behavior occur?
- **Context of situation:** What is going on at the time the behavior occurs? Is it during mealtime, bedtime, getting up in the morning, getting ready for school, prior to devotions or church time, when with certain peers or caregivers or some other time?

- **Diagnosis of any mental illness or disorder:** Are there signs of a serious mental health problem—mood swings, hallucinations, depression, anxiety?
- **History of trauma:** It is important to have the *story* of each child in placement. We need to know what type of trauma was experienced, length of time, severity, and the reaction to that trauma. (See section on Understanding Childhood Trauma, chapter 10.)
- **Prior behaviors and symptoms:** Have this or any similar behavior been a problem in the past?

Definitions of Behavior

- **Verbal or physical aggression:** verbal threats or physically attacking staff or others
- **Rage:** verbal or physical episodes of severe anger, which is out of control, which might be just yelling and screaming or as severe as to involve property destruction and harming others
- **Fighting/arguing:** starting physical or verbal conflicts, creating chaos in the home
- **Biting:** self or others, not during a rage
- **Boundary violations:** going to rooms of others where not permitted, interrupting, bossing about others, trying to control the house
- **Oppositional and defiant behavior:** this is basically doing the opposite of what is requested, acting in a passive-aggressive manner, verbally complying with a request but then just sitting there; anger and irritability are common, and this stems from high internal anger state.
- **Lying:** not being truthful, not coming up with the real story when something happens, story keeps changing, and so forth; many caregivers lessen consequences once the child is truthful about what he or she did—this is generally considered appropriate
- **Stealing:** may be from peers, staff, school, or community
- **Disobedience:** often a consequence of not doing well with gaining trust, associated with oppositional behaviors
- **Runaway:** need to know if running *from* the home or *to* something outside the home, often due to attachment crisis
- **Suicidal threats:** making statements that he or she wants to end his life, doesn't want to wake up tomorrow, or that God would just take him or her home now, up to having a plan as to how to complete a suicide; must be evaluated

carefully—there are levels of threats, which require varying levels of vigilance (see chapter 18, Suicidal and Self-Destructive Behavior)

- **Inappropriate elimination:** feces or urine put in places they should not be, includes finger painting with feces, which is associated with neglect and poor attachment
- **Self-cutting, erasing, scratching:** can become quite addictive and problematic, using an eraser particularly seems to be associated with a desire to not be around; suicidal thoughts must be evaluated at that point; define how much cutting or scratching occurred; is it deep enough to require medical attention? Cutting is not always suicidal. In the process of cutting, there is acute pain which releases endorphins in the brain which are like morphine which is an opiate. There is a calming effect, even a sort of high, that can make the behavior addictive.
- **Crying:** can be a sign of depression or used for manipulation, something that might have worked well in the past
- **Fears:** define the particular fears and in what context; often fears are related to trauma or are from a high anxiety level
- **Panic:** a high level of anxiety associated with sometimes suicidal thoughts, wanting to run away, may be due to trauma or an anxiety disorder; panic comes in attacks lasting up to several hours and are very uncomfortable, more of a medical issue than behavior but needs to be defined
- **Screaming:** can be manipulative, part of the trauma reaction or result of a developmental disorder; look at context and what rewards are provided
- **Sexual talk:** bringing up sexual themes in public, with peers, indicating that it is something they are thinking about a good deal; if child is coming from the street, it is just part of his vocabulary but needs to be addressed—trauma history is important
- **Sexual threats:** more serious but still verbal, generally something that peers will report and should be encouraged to report
- **Sexual activity:** define level of activity and context—what, where, when, how; care and consideration needs to be taken to determine if you are able to keep this child out of trouble and keep others safe from him in order to allow him/her in your home/facility
- **Talking back:** lack of respect, speaking to adults in a way in which the child is exerting control
- **Property destruction:** not rage related, might be her own things or those of another, which also becomes a boundary violation

- **Eating nonfood items:** known as *pica*, related to some vitamin deficiencies, needs medical evaluation; might also be deemed defiant behavior after analyzing context
- **Hoarding food (or other item):** taking leftovers or food from a meal, stealing from kitchen to store in her room
- **Other behaviors:** children seem to come up with new and different behaviors; find a good name for it so that others understand what you are talking about

Context

- **Were there any provocative factors?** Question what might have led to the behavior and how that might relate to the circumstance.
- **Who, where, what, when, and how?** Investigate the whole picture when you can, looking at timing and sequence of events.
- **Was the approach of the caregiver provocative?** Examine whether or not the responder did or said something that might have provoked the incident. It is necessary that we remain humble and apt to learn from our own mistakes, making it easier to figure things out sometimes.
- **Was the approach of the caregiver different?** If something fundamental changed in the way the child was approached, this might have assisted with making it a bit worse.
- **Did the consequences from prior behaviors provoke current problem?** Even if the consequences were not overdone, the reaction to them might be. The next approach might have to be modified to assist with not provoking even more problems. (An example might be that of a seriously abused child with an undesired behavior, which provokes the reaction in the caregiver of yelling at the child. The caregiver, unaware of this part of her history, does not know that this is just how her stepfather yelled at her prior to being beaten or raped.)
- **Is the child reacting the same way as before?** It might be time for a change in approach, as something is not working.

Root Cause Analysis

It sounds complicated and technical, but you can do it! This is about using the tools you are learning in this manual to think about what is happening so you can design a better approach. Many times, it helps to answer the *why*. When we understand the why (as in the above situation), behavior can change to better deal with the situation.

- Behaviors that are not responding to usual approaches or consequences require more thought and can benefit from root cause analysis.
- Root cause analysis is a procedure in which we analyze the behavior in terms of type of behavior, context, and probable causative factors.
- Based on these factors, we are better able to design a more informed approach to deal with the behavior or symptom.
- It is best to undertake the analysis with other staff members so you can put your heads together for more brainpower.

Sometimes, when we take time to analyze a situation to discover what is the root cause, the results can be surprising and rewarding. In one orphanage in Latin America, I was informed that the teenagers were basically in a mutiny. All twenty-one had decided that they wanted to leave, and to leave NOW! I called an emergency meeting with all of the teens and their houseparents to hear them out. The children were upset about nearly everything. They complained about how they were treated. How some of their peers were bullying, how some would not talk to them, and how everything was just not good. "We are done, we just want to leave," they said repeatedly. I dismissed the children to meet with staff separately to discover a bit more of what was happening. In exploring the situation, the houseparents revealed that they had taken a decision to retire (after eighteen years) from their positions. They indicated that they were just emotionally exhausted after all the years. I explored with them the attitudes that they had toward the children, and they were able to see that they had already emotionally withdrawn from them, no longer instilling the energy of caring that had been a major part of their ministering to these children. My thought was that these children, who mostly had been already abandoned on the street or by the death or disappearance of their biological parents, were experiencing, maybe, a sense of abandonment by the houseparents. I reconvened the group with the teens. I first had the houseparents disclose to them that they were going to retire in a few months from their role but would still be serving in a different capacity. This evoked some emotion. However, when I proposed to them that maybe they were starting to feel the abandonment that they felt prior to coming to the orphanage, this opened a floodgate of emotions. I allowed them to process this for some time before I asked them to disband for the night so that they could consider their decision to leave, and we would meet again at breakfast. They slowly left the dining hall where we were meeting and went back to their rooms. I spent time talking with the houseparents, who by this time were rather emotional themselves. After about an hour, one by one, the teens started coming back. One spoke for them all: "We want to apologize to Mom and Dad for our behavior." This was not expected but did not stop there. The children started addressing each other, asking forgiveness for various things that really no one knew were going on. The emotions from the prior session were nothing compared to this; tears were freely flowing (from myself, the staff, and the houseparents as well). It took some time, but after midnight, we finally closed in a long prayer, hugs, and good nights. The attitude in that house was transformed, and the behaviors changed once we were able to see what the actual issues were.

It made all the difference when we backed off and considered the ROOT CAUSE of the problems!

Diagnoses and Behaviors

- Children in care are at a high risk for suffering from a mental illness or developmental disorder that can affect behaviors and adjustments.
- Each disorder has its own unique symptoms and resulting behaviors.
- Some of the usual consequences for behaviors might actually worsen certain types of behaviors.
- Understanding the particular diagnosis, related behaviors, and more appropriate approaches can serve to better meet the needs of a particular child.

Post-Traumatic Stress Disorder

- Triggers are defined as sights, smells, tones of voice, sounds, places, or sensations such as touching that are related to a prior trauma and serve to bring up memories or flashbacks about the trauma. These might unexpectedly lead to sudden aggression, runaway, oppositional behavior, or bizarre reactions.
- Specific fears due to triggers might cause avoidance interpreted as oppositional behavior.
- Flashbacks are vivid audiovisual reenactments of a prior trauma. They might occur from exposure to a trigger (see above). They can cause many types of reactions, which could be interpreted as bad behavior—yelling, screaming, panic, avoidance, fear of certain people or places, overreactions to situations, crying, assuming a fetal position, or hiding.
- Sexualized behaviors can occur from triggers or from just normal interaction with peers. This is dealt with more in chapter 11, Sexual Abuse and Sexualized Children.

- If a child is hypersensitive to some types of touch or hugs, learn the particulars of that child, what he can and cannot tolerate, and moderate your own behavior accordingly.
- If a child is severely traumatized, there might be episodes of dissociation in which the child truly does not recall what was happening during the behavior. This is triggered by a traumatic memory, usually provoked by an event that reminds her of the trauma. More information is found in chapter 10, Understanding Childhood Trauma.

Bipolar Disorder

This is a mood disorder in which there is cycling of mood from high to low energy states, as the brain is unable to keep the moods in a stable place. Manic moods can be high energy, hyperactive, overly happy, irritable, angry, or paranoid. Depressive moods can be low energy, sad, apathetic, or irritable.

- Manic behavior might be impulsive, hyperactive, and intense but not able to be well controlled by the child.
- Depressive behavior might include resistance, oppositional behavior, negative self-statements, suicidal behavior, or cutting.
- Rapid mood swings might serve to produce irritability and rage, both physical and verbal.

Anxiety Disorders

- **Obsessive-compulsive behaviors.** Obsessions are recurrent unwanted thoughts or worries. Compulsions are behaviors that try to undo the obsessions. If there is a worry about germs, the compulsion is to excessively clean the environment or wash oneself.
- **Panic.** This is a sudden attack of severe anxiety, increased heart rate, sweating, intense fear, with possible accompanying suicidal thoughts. It is important not to confuse this with negative behaviors. This is real distress and very uncomfortable.
- **Avoidance.** The child might avoid places or crowds due to a high level of anxiety.
- **Irritability.** The child is easily upset when demands are placed, as he or she cannot naturally cope well with stress. Make sure you are not presenting too much, which might overwhelm the child and actually provoke the behaviors.

- **Intolerance of change.** Changing circumstances or routine might cause resistance and discomfort. The child needs a bit of warning before major events or change is going to occur.

Asperger Syndrome (Autism Spectrum Disorder)

- **Intolerance to change.** These children carry a very high anxiety level and do poorly when routines are changed. Change might induce a panic or melt-down, including anger, crying, or other loss of emotional control.
- **Fixations.** The child tends to have certain things he gets stuck on to the point that much else is excluded. Attempts to change the behavior might be met with resistance, oppositional behavior, aggression, or meltdown. As you learn the ways of the child, you will discover ways to avoid the meltdowns, making life much better for them.
- **Intense interests.** The child often has a hobby or academic interest that excludes all else, becoming somewhat of an expert in the subject. It helps to allow him to share the interest from time to time, with limits.
- **Intolerance to certain foods, materials, situations.** A child might have tac-tile hypersensitivity—that is, he does not like to be touched, he or she avoids certain clothing materials, and the textures of certain foods bother them.
- **Overreactions to noises, confusion.** Some might have hypersensitive hearing, which is at a much higher frequency than most of us. This can lead to overreaction in a store or in crowds. Learning the way of the child again is important. Many of these traits are more severe when not yet attached, and most decrease in intensity as the child matures.
- **Irrational fears.** This might come from the fixations or a fantasy life.
- **Impulsive speech.** A child might say what he is thinking without having regard to the situation and whether it might be inappropriate.
- **Hypersensitivity to touch.** Some do not tolerate hugs or even hand-to-shoulder contact but can gradually adapt.

Reactive Attachment Disorder

- **Hoarding food or other items.** Abandoned or neglected children, for fear of not having sufficient food, will steal and hoard food items. Approach this with a gentle, supportive manner that reassures there is enough and that the child will be taken care of.

- **Stealing.** There is not a sense of ownership that comes with normal development. With patience, we teach it. The behavior must still have consequences.
- **Rages.** These can be verbal or physical, often coming during the expected attachment crisis, and can be very useful to assist with attachment. The rage is often directed at the mother, as this is who they might subconsciously feel betrayed them. See chapter 5, Reactive Attachment Disorder.
- **Fear of intimacy.** This is a result of overreaction to situations that remind the child of family relationships or people in the family who betrayed him, often the mother. As attachment proceeds, the child gradually learns to love and connect with others.
- **Lack of boundaries.** Without developmental attachment, the sense of self is not well developed. There is not an understanding of "what is yours is yours, and what is mine is mine."
- **Overreaction to certain types of touch.** Be sensitive to each child's patterns and comfort level.

As mentioned in the treatment of RAD, which you are involved in constantly, be aware that certain behaviors the child presents are intended to make you react in one of two ways: (1) to draw you closer or (2) to push you away. This is called *distancing* and *approximating*. It has to do with the struggles of attachment. Today, she wants to be close to you, follow you around, and help out where she can. Tomorrow, she is a handful, doing the very things she knows will get on your last nerve. What is happening? While drawing close to you, she becomes panicked about making a real connection: "Maybe I should still be connected to my natural mother or my sister. If I like you a lot, I am betraying them." If you understand the struggle, you can more effectively address and understand the behavior. Sometimes, just a reassuring word will calm a child down. It is not possible to really talk to her about this, as she does understand why she does these things. The reason for these behaviors is complex, having to do with divided loyalties and fear of rejection, fear of intimacy, fear of being emotionally or physically hurt, and anger toward those who betrayed the child. These are the main issues in the confused and hurting heart of the child.

Spiritual Issues

An area we cannot overlook is the area of spiritual influence on behavior. As we gather the history of the children in our care, some will have a spiritual history that may possibly indicates some demonic involvement. This is expected; Satan has claimed these children for himself. He has no compassion and will use the little children as his pawns just as he uses adults who will commit to him. I have included a section on spiritual warfare that can be consulted when needed for these issues.

Signs of Spiritual Problems

- Avoidance of the Bible
- Irreverence, constantly taking God's name in vain
- Dissociative behaviors, clearly not recalling what he had done
- Hypnotic trances in which words or phrases are repeated
- Voices, especially ones with names and personalities that control him
- Horrific visions and nightmares
- Nightmares and visions are worse if attending church or having devotions
- History of involvement in satanic cults or similar local religions (Haitian voodoo, various cults in Mexico, animism in Africa, native Hawaiian religion, etc.)

See chapter 17, Spiritual Warfare, to address this, but do not try to address it alone.

Conclusion

When behaviors do not respond, then what?

- Start the thinking process.
- Look at the history of the child.
- Consider the context of the behaviors.
- Bring the situation to a staff meeting or supervisor.
- When necessary, pass on information to doctors, social workers, or therapists.
- Design an informed modified approach together as staff, including the child if appropriate in the given situation.
- The approach, in some cases, might include therapy and medication. In some cases, spiritual warfare is needed.

- Through the process, we continue actively loving the child unconditionally (agape love).
- Always keep in mind that the goal of managing the behaviors is to teach them how to become ***productive Christian adults.***

Notes

6

Making Disciples

To meet the goal of bringing the children up in Christ and to be His followers as productive Christian adults, we need to *disciple* them, which basically is attracting them to follow Christ and learn from His Word.

> Therefore, go and make disciples of all nations, baptizing them in the name of the Father and of the Son and of the Holy Spirit, and teaching them to obey everything I have commanded you. And surely, I am with you always, to the very end of the age.
>
> —Matthew 28:19

"If you want to shape a person's life," wrote researcher George Barna in *Transforming Children into Spiritual Champions* (Ventura CA: Regal, 2003) "whether you are most concerned about his or her moral, spiritual, intellectual, emotional or economic development—it is during these crucial eight years [from ages five to twelve] that lifelong habits, values, beliefs, and attitudes are formed."

If children have a clear and proper exposure to the Good News of Jesus, they are remarkably receptive. There's no time to waste, for a person's conscious spiritual and moral development starts as early as age two—maybe even earlier, much earlier. The moral foundations are generally determined before age ten. "By age nine," wrote Barna, "most children have their spiritual moorings in place." By thirteen, a person's spiritual identity is largely established.

"If you want to have a lasting influence upon the world," wrote Barna, "you must invest in people's lives; and if you want to maximize that investment, then you must invest in those people while they are young...Children matter to God because He loves them and wants them to experience the best, right from the start of their lives."

First Steps

- Priority One: Your Relationship with Christ
- Your mission statement: What are you here for? As we serve Him, we need to understand why we are here and what is our purpose and calling. If you are called to serve in a children's ministry, then what is your personal goal following the main goal of establishing and maintaining a strong relationship with Christ?
- **Designing a focus for ministry:** Put the mission statement into action. Once we have designed our own mission statement, we can put it into action so that we can be effective servants of the Most High God.
- **Walking the talk, talking the walk:** We must do both to be effective.
- **Living and working as a servant of the Most High God:** Our service as His servant then becomes our daily life's purpose.

Walking the Talk

- Teaching as a way of life
- All that you do is an example
- Admitting mistakes
- Seeking forgiveness
- Forgiving
- Demonstrating compassion
- Loving the unlovely
- Reaching out to the undesirable
- Giving generously
- Maintaining a positive attitude
- Showing humility
- Showing reverence for the holy
- Refraining from gossip

- Demonstrating priorities
- Active listening
- Love in action

What are other ways you can walk the talk?
"Preach the gospel always, use words when necessary." wrote St. Francis of Assisi. Words are often necessary but are much more effective when backed by action.

> You are the salt of the earth. But if the salt loses its saltiness, how can it be made salty again? It is no longer good for anything, except to be thrown out and trampled underfoot. You are the light of the world. A town build on a hill cannot be hidden. Neither do people light a lamp and put it under a bowl. Instead they put it on its stand, and it gives light to everyone in the house. In the same way, let your light shine before others, that they may see your good deeds and glorify your Father in heaven.
>
> —Matthew 5:13–16

Talking the Walk

> These are the commands, decrees and laws the Lord your God directed me to teach you to observe in the land that you are crossing the Jordan to possess, so that you, your children and their children after them may fear the Lord your God as long as you live by keeping all his decrees and commands that I give you, and so that you may enjoy long life. Hear, Israel, and be careful to obey so that it may go well with you and that you may increase greatly in a land flowing with milk and honey, just as the Lord, the God of your ancestors, promised you. Hear, O Israel: The Lord our God, the Lord is one. Love the Lord your God with all your heart and with all your soul and with all your strength. These commandments that I give you today are to be on your hearts. Impress them on your children. Talk about them when you sit at home and when you walk along the road, when you lie down and when you get up. Tie them as symbols on your hands and bind them on your foreheads. Write them on the doorframes of your houses and on your gates.
>
> —Deuteronomy 6:1–9

- The teacher teaches in all circumstances—we are always teaching! Make sure what you are teaching is based in good values.
- Find the moments throughout each day in which something can be taught through example or words.

- Know the facts, stay in the Word, and keep yourself close to the Savior and His teachings.
- Discipline is an opportunity to show love and teach what Jesus would want in the situation. It is a teachable moment of which we can take advantage.
- Use words to encourage, instruct, uplift, love, express care, correct, calm, and that honor Jesus. Use words to share your life with the child.

> But the wisdom that comes from heaven is first of all pure; then peace-loving, considerate, submissive, full of mercy and good fruit, impartial and sincere. Peacemakers who sow in peace reap a harvest of righteousness.
>
> —James 3:17–18

Some words from a popular song by Steve Green say it all:

> We're pilgrims on the journey
> Of the narrow road
> And those who've gone before us line the way
> Cheering on the faithful, encouraging the weary
> Their lives a stirring testament to God's sustaining grace
> But as those who've gone before us
> Let us leave to those behind us
> The heritage of faithfulness passed on through godly lives
>
> www.stevegreenministries.org

Leading a Child to Christ

The hopeful outcome of our efforts to demonstrate our faith is that we come to a point that the child wants to accept Jesus as his personal savior. This is a personal decision, one that cannot be forced. It must be taken seriously and appropriate steps taken when the child is ready. A useful guide for this is found at: http://www.cefbook-ministry.com/downloads/ucan4lead.pdf

This is a pdf file of a book called *U Can Lead Children to Christ* by Dr. Sam Doherty,

The basics are the ABCs.

The child must be able to

- **A**cknowledge that he or she is a sinner,
- **B**elieve that Jesus died and rose again and has paid for our sins, and
- **C**onfess that Jesus is Lord and so accept him as his or her personal savior.

Here are some suggested verses:

- ***Acknowledge***
  Romans 3:23: For all have sinned and fall short of the glory of God.
  Romans 6:23: For the wages of sin is death, but the gift of God is eternal life in Christ Jesus our Lord.
- ***Believe***
  Acts 16:31: They replied, "Believe in the Lord Jesus, and you will be saved—you and your household.
  Romans 10:17: Consequently, faith comes from hearing the message, and the message is heard through the word about Christ.
- ***Confess***
  Romans 10:9–11: If you declare with your mouth, "Jesus is Lord," and believe in your heart that God raised him from the dead, you will be saved. For it is with your heart that you believe and are justified, and it is with your mouth that you profess your faith and are saved. As Scripture says, "Anyone who believes in him will never be put to shame."
  Consequently, faith comes from hearing the message, and the message is heard through the word about Christ.
  Acts 2:38–39: Peter replied, "Repent and be baptized, every one of you, in the name of Jesus Christ for the forgiveness of your sins. And you will receive the gift of the Holy Spirit. The promise is for you and your children and for all who are far off—for all whom the Lord our God will call."

Once the child has prayed to receive the Lord, the scripture states that the believer's baptism is the next step. However, the journey is only beginning. Now, with the gift of the Holy Spirit, the child has more power to resist temptation and do those things that please and glorify God.

In Summary

We must be all about Passing the Faith Along

- *By walking the talk*
- *By talking the walk*
- *By living the Word*

In order to be salt and light in the lives of the children.

It Takes More Than Love—It Takes Agape Love.

Notes

7

A Word about Boundaries

The existence of *boundaries* is very important in the structure of a healthy family home as well as in a foster home or children's home. With well-defined boundaries, we have a house in which there is individual respect, security, and the opportunity to teach values and morals, improve self-esteem, and integrate structure in the lives of the children served. Without boundaries, a lack of structure can result in chaos that might include disrespect, insecurity, theft, deceit, cheating, and nonexistent personal rights.

For boundaries in the home to be well understood by the children, we must teach by example. Those who are raised in a traditional healthy family will have the natural opportunity to internalize the family's structure and have well-defined boundaries. The children who arrive later in the home have not had the opportunity to learn the family boundaries and therefore might present with problems of stealing others' property, borrowing with no intention of returning, destroying personal property, or fighting and arguing. Teaching boundaries in the home is a priority.

Qualities of Healthy Boundaries

- Based on LOVE: 1 Corinthians 13:4–8a

  Love is patient, love is kind. It does not envy, it does not boast, it is not proud. It does not dishonor others, it is not self-seeking, it is not easily angered, it keeps no record of wrongs. Love does not delight in evil but rejoices with the truth. It always protects, always trusts, always hopes, always perseveres. Love never fails. (NIV)

- Fair rules and appropriate consequences
- Respect for others
- Holding others in high regard
- Maintaining personal space, rules of courtesy
- Understanding what is mine and what belongs to the other person:
  - possessions
  - feelings
  - responsibilities
  - authority
  - accountability
  - body parts

Knowing my own limits:

- that I am a fallible human
- that I can be tempted and can fall
- that if I lack a strong relationship with Christ, Satan will use and destroy me

Maintaining Boundaries

1. Be *humble* and listen to what others, including the children, say. We cannot change or correct ourselves if we have pride. Recognize that you are fallible and can be led astray.
2. Understand that the children who are under our protection have not had well-defined boundaries in their lives.
3. Avoid situations in which you find yourself alone with a child of the opposite sex; especially in the case of sexualized children, be careful how you interact even with the same sex.

   — *Counseling*: Private talks with the children need to be with a caregiver of the same sex, if possible. If not, they must take place in a location where others can see without hearing.
   — *Transporting*: Never have a male staffer alone with a female child, and vice versa, unless accompanied by at least one other staff member.
4. At times, the children need to talk about personal topics—sex, body issues, menstruation, or other private matters. It is very important that these topics be discussed with the caregiver of the same sex, in a private place, and that the proper information is provided, although only what is needed at the moment.
5. Maintain respect for the property of the children. There are reasons to search a room when there are suspicious behaviors suspicious, such as drug use, Satanism, pornography, evidence of thievery, and so forth. The search should occur with the child present, with or without her permission. In cases of possible danger to self or others, such as suicidal or homicidal threats, it will then be necessary to search the room with or without the child present, no permission from the child necessary.
6. Respect the personal space of the children. If there is no desire for a hug or touch, refrain from doing so. Do not force hugs or sustained eye contact. Maintain common courtesy in the home by asking permission, saying "please" and "thank you," and using proper greetings and salutations.

Notes

8

Creating a Confident Child

A strong desire of parents is that their child would not only grow into a productive Christian adult but that they grow in confidence in themselves, understanding who they are and what they are capable of. Having confidence supplies resilience. Resilience gives us a better chance to withstand the pressures of life, do well in our chosen professions, and truly become what God wants us to become. The world teaches our children that we are but a product of random collection of molecules. Somehow, out of primordial ooze, animals and people developed over billions of years. We have no purpose other than to reproduce and survive. We are no better than animals. Some even propose we are less than the animals and are really destroying their planet. That does not provide much of a foundation to build a life on.

People often talk of self-esteem and self-image. What are they?

Self-esteem is really how we regard ourselves, descriptive adjectives mostly, how much of what I am. For example: I may say "I am a really good at math," and if the truth is you really are, that would be a realistic self-esteem. A good self-esteem most closely matches what is real. I can be overconfident and say that I am a great scientist, and really, I am mediocre;

that would be poor self-esteem as it is not realistic. I might say I am a really bad artist, but my work is very good. That would also be a poor self-esteem, as I am not regarding the truth about myself.

Self-image is all about who I am. My race, my gender, my liabilities, my assets, my roots, my family identity, my appearance, my position in Christ, all the other descriptors of who I *really* am. A good self-image most closely matches what is real and true. In effect, how God sees us.

If we start with the foundation that the world gives us, we are basing our lives on a lie, thus the foundation is very unstable. We have to create a sense of purpose which is based on nothing but human opinion.

In this paradigm, the purpose might be:

To be happy.
To work hard and provide for my family.
To have fun.
To make a lot of money and have more toys than anyone else.
To be successful (which is not well-defined).
To get all you can out of life, you only go around once.

The world is also teaching our children that they can be whatever they want to be regardless of what they are endowed with. If you are a boy and want to be a girl, you can decide that. If you are a girl and want to be a boy, a doctor will help you change.

Looking at all of the above, we can see that if we base our lives on those desires, we are going to be disappointed. If we want to be something other than what God, our designer, planned for us, we will also be quite distressed and discouraged. Basing our lives on these things can lead to distress, discouragement, depression, anxiety, suicidal thoughts, or even destruction of our very lives.

If we honestly look down deep inside to find our meaning, we will only find sin and darkness if we are not a child of God. We really fall short of even standards the world might set but especially the standards of God in His word. Looking deep inside as a child of God, we see that we are imperfect sinners but redeemed, paid for forgiveness, and made righteous.

Building our life on the crumbling foundation of the world gives the child no confidence, no purpose, no direction, and no certain destiny.

If a child's life is built on the strong foundation of the Word of God, they can base their self-concept and self-esteem on what God says, which does not change. We must address these questions so that we can assist in building proper self-concept.

Let's look at some ways we can help the child to arrive at a good sense of self:

Starting with who I really am:

> Ephesians chapter 1 states the following: (vv. 1–14)
>
> Paul, an apostle of Christ Jesus by the will of God,
>
> To God's holy people in Ephesus, the faithful in Christ Jesus:
> Grace and peace to you from God our Father and the Lord Jesus Christ.
> Praise be to the God and Father of our Lord Jesus Christ, who has blessed us in the heavenly realms with every spiritual blessing in Christ. For he chose us in him before the creation of the world to be holy and blameless in his sight. In love he predestined us for adoption to sonship through Jesus Christ, in accordance with his pleasure and will—to the praise of his glorious grace, which he has freely given us in the One he loves. In him we have redemption through his blood, the forgiveness of sins, in accordance with the riches of God's grace that he lavished on us. With all wisdom and understanding, he made known to us the mystery of his will according to his good pleasure, which he purposed in Christ, to be put into effect when the times reach their fulfillment—to bring unity to all things in heaven and on earth under Christ.
> In him we were also chosen, having been predestined according to the plan of him who works out everything in conformity with the purpose of his will, in order that we, who were the first to put our hope in Christ, might be for the praise of his glory. And you also were included in Christ when you heard the message of truth, the gospel of your salvation. When you believed, you were marked in him with a seal, the promised Holy Spirit, who is a deposit guaranteeing our inheritance until the redemption of those who are God's possession—to the praise of his glory.

From the above, we learn if we have accepted Christ and are children of God:

- We were chosen by God before the world was created to be holy and blameless in His sight.
- He adopted us and sons through Jesus Christ.
- He freely gave His Son Jesus who gave Himself that we could be His forever.
- We have redemption through his blood and we are forgiven of all our sins.

- We were chosen to be for the praise of His glory.
- We were marked with a seal guaranteeing our inheritance in Him.

What is my purpose in life?

To serve and worship the King.

As we worship and draw close to Him, he provides us the purpose and direction in our lives.

If we delight in Him, he will fulfill the desires of our heart

Ps 137:4–6

Take delight in the Lord,
and he will give you the desires of your heart.
Commit your way to the Lord;
trust in him and he will do this:
He will make your righteous reward shine like the dawn, your vindication like the noonday sun.

That is, He will show us what our desires really are and fulfill those desires. That gives us true satisfaction and peace.

The Word of God provides our foundation. The building blocks in that foundation are the following:

Origin
Purpose/Meaning
Morality
Destiny

By building on these blocks, we can help the child to be secure in his/her beliefs, have confidence in God, and know really who they are in Christ.

How can we build on these blocks?

Origin: Using the Genesis story of Creation, talk about how the world really came about. Science believes differently, but they were not there, God was. Anything that disagrees with God's word will, at some point, be disproven as has most of the evolution theories. Genesis talks of a six-day creation week; there is no reason to doubt what God has presented. Find opportunities to create awe regarding the creative power of God and relate that to the child having been created in His image and is special to Him.

Purpose/Meaning: Using the stories in the Bible of praise and evangelism as well as the psalms of praising to God. Our lives are empty without God. We have a God-shaped vacuum in our hearts that only He can fill. We were made to praise and glorify Him. We do that in our work, our home, at school, at church, and anywhere we might go. That is our real purpose; anything else will not fill that void in our hearts.

Morality: What is God's plan for how we should live, and why does it work better? Use real-life examples of how people have failed terribly by not following Christ in their lives: murder, drugs, divorce, deception, stealing, every kind of evil that we can or cannot imagine. Following God's rules helps keep the world a better place to live. Who started hospitals, clinics, outreach to orphans, widows, often the first to arrive at a disaster? God's people.

Destiny: Where will I go when I am done living here on earth? Many have searched for answers, but only the Bible provides the absolute answer, whether we like it or not. As children of God, we have a home in heaven, an inheritance with Christ, and in reality, we are his inheritance! How wonderful is that! It seems we talk about heaven mostly at funerals, but it is a subject we can talk about any time and get excited about it!

With these basic foundational blocks, the child can realistically begin the journey of self-discovery. I know now who I am, where I come from, where I am headed, and who sets the rules, so how do I fit in?

We must help the child to see himself as God sees him, realistic. I am a boy that is unchangeable, or I am a girl that is unchangeable. What are my interests? Hobbies? What talents do I have? When a special gift is noted, be it music, writing, math, science, manual dexterity, whatever it might be, you help the child to further develop that ability with encouragement and maybe some extra challenges in the area they seem to be able to do well in.

We affirm the gender identity with male activities for the boys and female activities for the girls but also noting there are a number of things that we specify are only for girls or for boys that really are not specific. A girl might enjoy working on machines or cars; a boy might have an interest in dancing and art. That does not mean they are not fitting in with their God-given gender. If there is confusion, they need to be affirmed in who they really are so that they can come to accept it if they are struggling with that.

Working with those children with unresolved attachment or with significant trauma history will struggle more with being able to accept themselves as someone worthy of love. Until that occurs, the work on self-image is very difficult. We however must always strive to help the child to develop the foundation of a healthy self-image, which is being able to see themselves as a beloved child of God, chosen and special in His sight and yours, created for the praise of His glory.

A child who has been immersed in the negative during their life prior to coming into placement with you will have certain beliefs about himself that will gradually change, but it will take time.

Strong Negative Beliefs

I am a bad person.
I cannot do anything right.
Nobody loves me.
Nobody cares for me.
There is no one who can help me. I have to do it all myself.
I am stronger than anyone else. I can beat them up

These beliefs often are communicated in challenging behaviors. If we understand the core beliefs of the child and work on changing those for those built on reality and the Word of God, we can see wonderful changes in the life of the child.

Learning through Failures

As parents/caregivers, we need to be always be on the lookout for teachable moments. This can even (or especially) happen when there is a failure. The child tries very hard, but their team does not win. Something happens in which they do not try but and lose, or make some big mistakes, or demonstrate some very difficult behaviors. As caregivers, our love is to be like God's love (not always easy), loving the sinner, hating the sin. We use the moment to help them learn something about themselves and encourage them in the proper direction.

These moments can be used to teach great lessons about always trying to do your best and can be moments in which you can help to change those core beliefs, those lies they believe about themselves.

Victors or Victims?

Many of these children have struggled with severe trauma, separation, rejection, and as a result, may have developed the sense of always being a victim. We need to recognize this in these children and gently work to change them into victors with an ***I can do it*** attitude. Using the metaphor of a ship, our past can be an anchor, always holding us back, or a rudder helping to guide us into a better future. In our teachable moments we need to always keep this in mind.

Creating a confident child then means that we help them see who they really are in Christ, build on their strengths and strengthen their weak areas so that they may become the best that they can.

Notes

The First Days

Helping the New Arrivals

To succeed with children coming into placement, it is necessary to start with the idea and goal of *success* but also to have on hand the tools and strategies necessary to lead them forward in their lives. We must start with high goals and hopes but also expectations that are reasonable. We leave our own predetermined ideas behind to give them the best chance to change their lives.

Gather all the information available about the children to best understand them and create a plan specific for each child.

History

Where did the child live prior to coming to the home—on the street, in a shelter, another orphanage, with family, with natural or adoptive parents, with a single mother?

- Approximately how many placements has the child been in since leaving natural parent or parents?

- Was there physical abuse, sexual abuse, or abandonment?
- What were the circumstances—death of parent or parents, drug-addicted or alcoholic parents, ill parents, or parents unable to care for the child?
- Does the child have health issues, previous or upcoming surgeries, chronic physical problems, or psychiatric care in the past or present?
- Are there family members who still care for the child and want to be involved?
- Has the child connected with anyone in the past after leaving home? Does he or she make friends or ask for help from caregivers?
- Are there indications of any developmental problems or intellectual disorder?
- The above comprises much of the *story* of the child, up to the point he or she comes to live with you. This story needs to be made into a permanent record so that all the caregivers have adequate knowledge of each child in care.
- At the end of this chapter is a handy outline for intake data that might be helpful in organizing useful information about the child.

Behaviors

From the information available, we can inform ourselves of the type of behaviors that might have been present prior to coming. With many government placements, the data is minimal in most countries. Possible behaviors might include any of the following:

Disobedience
Rebellion
Talking back
Excessive crying
Fearful anxiety
Depression
Sexualized behaviors
Controlling or bullying
Symptoms of a serious mental illness, such as hearing voices, paranoia, believing things that are not true, seeing things not present
Unusual or bizarre behaviors
Behaviors suggestive of serious spiritual issues (see chapter 18, Spiritual Warfare)

Approaches

Depending on the history, we can modify our approaches accordingly. We can use what the child has experienced to inform the correct initial approach. This needs to be carefully considered so as to enhance a successful outcome.

Children from the street, depending how long they have been living that way, often do not understand tenderness or compassion and so may be quite suspicious of this and tend to distance themselves. This calls for a calm, fairly strict approach, emphasizing rules, as well as acceptance. Physical touch will likely be rejected initially, but as they begin to adapt, they may, in time, acclimate to touch and positive feelings.

Those who come from a background of physical abuse are likely going to fear the male staffers more than the female if the abuser was male and vice versa. Approach these children cautiously, checking to see how much closeness can be tolerated and how they react to hugs and touch.

Those who were sexually abused must be approached with care. They generally do not understand boundaries or normal human interactions. They tend to sexualize hugs and touches, becoming sexually aroused by the interaction. It is essential to be vigilant and to initiate the process of teaching them proper boundaries.

Those who have experienced a severe loss or succession of losses, such as death of parents, siblings, war trauma, or loss of home and family structure, are in the midst of grief and need a good deal of understanding, affection, and support. They also might not be able to trust or confide in you at first.

Those who come from a situation of abandonment will not easily accept affection in the beginning but can learn to trust more rapidly than those damaged by a history of abuse.

The First Day

The first impression is crucial for the new arrivals. It is *very* important to learn their names first. Before introducing them to the others in the house, it is good to separate them for a few moments for introduction. This is a suggested sequence:

1. Explore their history briefly, a few moments only.
2. Review the rules of the house, consequences, rewards, and daily schedule. You can impart a good deal of information at this point, not for the purpose that they learn and understand all of it, but for conveying a message that this home has structure.

3. With firmness, explain the expectations, such as good behavior, as well as school and worship attendance. Also, explain that the caregivers are going to do all they can to help them succeed but that they also have to put forth effort to make it work.
4. Finish the session with something positive, giving them encouragement to put forth their best efforts in the home.
5. Introduce them to the others and give them a tour of the house.
6. If they are able to read, it is OK to provide a written schedule with perhaps some rules and expectations.

What Follows

As discussed previously, during the process of attachment, the child normally passes through a "honeymoon" period in which there are attempts by the child to recruit the caregivers to care for him and connect. The child will try to do everything just right, trying to please the caregivers, obeying, speaking well, and being polite. Sometimes, this will not endure. The honeymoon can last up to three months on average, rarely longer. It might only be an hour or two. Some children start out with minimal problems, have only mild crises, and proceed to make good attachment. Others may struggle for several years and still turn out well.

Successful attachment requires willing and capable participants on both ends, the child and the one or ones he or she will attach to. Both need to be available to make the connection and have the capability to complete the task. The more failed attachment attempts the child has made, the more difficult it is to make a secure attachment. For most of the children in out-of-home placement, corrective attachment is likely given a safe, secure environment and capable, loving caregivers.

At around the three-month mark of placement, the child comes to a point in which he tests the caregivers' commitment, pushes limits, and might demonstrate very dis-agreeable behaviors. If the caregivers can confront the crisis and help the child through it, the next crisis will very likely not be as intense. Crises often occur periodically around every three months for a while. Every child is different—some might have only one major crisis, while others continue to have occasional crises until they are grown. Crises can include emotional episodes, crying, screaming, mood swings, and anger. They might consist of very disagreeable behaviors as though designed to make you very upset. Keeping your own emotions in check and dealing with the situation in a matter-of-fact way helps everyone get through the situation. This is often due to an attachment crisis, so negotiating through it allows attachment to proceed in a healthy manner.

As we work through the crises, the ups and downs, and are able to keep our unconditional love for the children and our energy strong, we can maintain high hopes for them and watch our expectations rise as they proceed with the process of attachment.

When Things Go Right

Sara was seven years old and living with her five-year-old sister, her four-year-old brother, and her two-year-old youngest brother. They were living with their mother, who was a street prostitute in Mexico City. Mother would go to work for days at a time and leave the children in the one-room apartment. If they tried to leave, the neighbor would beat them with a broom to keep them in the house. Sara would sneak out at night to try to find them food and hoped not to get beaten in the process.

One day, Mother left and just did not come back. Sara was getting desperate, as she could not get enough food for the baby. Finally, someone reported them to the police. The local child-protection workers were able to take them and place them in a government shelter for a few days. They were then moved to a Christian children's home on the outskirts of the city. This is where I met them.

They were frightened and very ill. The five-year-old was so full of worms that when she was treated, she developed severe pulmonary complications and nearly died. As they settled into the home, it became clear that they were not going to connect with anyone. They stayed apart from the caregivers and spent a lot of time talking with each other but not with the other children in the home.

After some months of the caregivers in the home trying to help them, they were brought in for counseling. I started with the oldest and had her tell me the entire story of what happened. I spent time with the others and made some connection with them, mostly playing with them. The next few times I met with the oldest again, after gaining her trust, she was able to tell me more of what had happened and how her life was prior to coming into care. I explained to her what was going on. She was forbidding her siblings from making any connections. She explained her fears and her loyalty to Mother, who had abandoned her. After a few very tearful sessions, she was starting to understand that she needed to give her siblings permission to attach to the caregivers in the home.

When she came in to the next session, I told her to look me in the eyes, I paused for a few seconds, then I told her sternly: "You are fired!"

She was rather shocked, so I explained to her she was no longer in the role of parent to her siblings, she could herself be a child. This was followed by a flood of tears, both of relief and sadness.

This was the turning point for them. The children began to attach and grow during the next several years. They had their problems, but the behaviors were just normal child behaviors. They all accepted Christ, dedicated their lives to him, and are currently serving in different ways. The youngest actually was able to develop a business while in high school that he was able to continue after he completed school. Their caregivers weathered the storms of attachment with them and survived many tough moments. They can look back in pride at how this family turned out.

On the following page is a suggested intake form that would have most of the information you really need to understand the child and get a good start, whether coming in as a foster child, a considered adoption, or being admitted to a residential children's facility or even for adoptive/foster placements.

INTAKE HISTORY FORM

NAME:

DATE OF BIRTH (or estimated age):

DATE OF ARRIVAL:

AGE WHEN LAST WITH A PARENT:

SOURCE OF REFERRAL:

TRIBE OR LANGUAGE GROUP:

RELIGION OF PARENTS:

CIRCUMSTANCES LEADING TO PLACEMENT:

PLACEMENT HISTORY:

TRAUMA HISTORY
(abuse, type of abuse, severity of abuse, war-related, accident, neglect, abandonment):

INFORMATION ABOUT PARENTS:

FAMILY HISTORY OF VIOLENCE, DRUGS, MENTAL ILLNESS, PHYSICAL ILLNESS:

MEDICAL HISTORY:

IMMUNIZATION HISTORY:

CURRENT MEDICATIONS:

WILL A PARENT OR RELATIVE REMAIN IN CONTACT?:

Notes

10

Understanding Childhood Trauma

But you, God, see the trouble of the afflicted; you consider their grief and take it in hand. The victims commit themselves to you; you are the helper of the fatherless.
—Psalm 10:14

Jesus the Great High Priest

"Therefore, since we have a great high priest who has ascended into heaven, Jesus the Son of God, let us hold firmly to the faith we profess. For we do not have a high priest who is unable to empathize with our weaknesses, but we have one who has been tempted in every way, just as we are—yet he did not sin. Let us then approach God's throne of grace with confidence, so that we may receive mercy and find grace to help us in our time of need." (Hebrews 4:14–16)

Most, if not all, children coming into care have experienced some level of trauma. They have at the very least suffered the trauma of not being able to live with their natural family. On the other end of the spectrum, they may have suffered beyond anything we could even imagine. Among the events in their young lives, some have been sexually abused, some have been physically abused, some have endured war, some have witnessed the effects of devastating illness or abandonment on the street of a major city or in the bush. Some may have witnessed the death of a parent or a terrible accident. Some may have been trafficked. Most have experienced at least some level of emotional abuse—all have had disruption of attachment.

Post-traumatic stress disorder (PTSD) occurs when trauma is severe enough to overwhelm the child's ability to cope and results in distressing symptoms or behaviors.

To more fully understand the effect of trauma on the child, take some time to review normal attachment and corrective attachment. You will recall from earlier chapters that there are some times in a child's development in which he or she is more vulnerable to the effects of trauma than at other times—those times when the child is transitioning from one stage of development to the next.

Review of Corrective Attachment

- Stages of attachment when successful in placement are similar to normal developmental process.
- Bonding, selective attachment, and attachment crises every three to four months.
- Three-year period to adequately correct attachment, but some problems might persist.

Review of Sexual Development

- Sexual stimulation prior to the brain being ready tends to short-circuit developing tracts, causing abnormal responses and confusion.
- Sexual stimulation with all the layers and tracts developed (that is when the person is emotionally and physically mature) is wholesome, tolerable, and healthy.

Developmental Vulnerability

- When each new stage of development is negotiated, at that point, the child is more vulnerable to the effects of trauma.
- Vulnerable stages include six months to nine months, fifteen months to twenty months, four years to six years, eleven years to fourteen years, seventeen years to nineteen years.

- Even adults can be more vulnerable to the effects of trauma at ages thirty-five to forty and sixty to sixty-five when negotiating the next stage of adult development.

Factors Related to the Trauma

To understand the effect of trauma, you must consider all contributing factors. The effect of trauma is a combination of duration, severity, and intensity of trauma on a vulnerable or resilient child who has or does not have family support or social supports in place.

Mild or Likely Inconsequential Trauma

- Touching of genitals through clothing a few times
- Single episode of direct touching
- Accidental touching or viewing of sexual activity but not repeatedly
- Occasional physical punishment acted out in rage
- Witnessing a minor accident or interpersonal violence of a short duration, no casualties

Moderate Intensity

- Repeated touching through the clothing
- Limited number of brief touching under the clothing
- Repeated viewing of nonviolent heterosexual pornographic material
- Repeated moderate physical abuse but with some positive support

Severe Intensity

- Repeated touching, without clothing, to point of orgasm
- Insertion of finger or penis into vagina or anus
- Rape with penetration by the penis or other object in the vagina or rectum
- Repeated viewing of sexual activity either pornographic or in real life
- Physical abuse to point of fearing for life on several occasions
- Accident or abuse independent of severity in which one believes life is in danger and reacts accordingly (overwhelming fear, terror)

- Viewing of severe trauma, such as finding your mother hanging, father shot to death, or severe accident of other close family member
- Repetitive threats to one's life by someone capable of perpetrating harm
- War-related trauma, viewing death and destruction from up close

Victim Factors

- Is child already a vulnerable child, suffering attachment disorder, mental disorder, or lack of family support?
- Has child previously endured trauma?
- Did support system believe the disclosure of trauma?
- Was child able to dissociate during the course of the abuse? Dissociation is basically blacking out during the event, mentally removing oneself from the trauma. It is still experienced, but that memory is isolated to another section of the memory bank, which might be hard to retrieve.
- Has the trauma led to symptom development or abnormal behaviors?
- Has the child begun to victimize others sexually or physically?
- Does the child regularly seek out an attachment figure when symptoms are present? This is positive and tends toward healing.

Symptom Formation

- Symptoms are dependent on developmental stage, vulnerability, and intensity and severity of trauma.
- Symptoms can be severe to point of very difficult to manage even in residential care.
- Sexual stimulation prior to the brain's readiness to adapt to the stimuli short-circuits the sexual response, causing confusion and can result in sexualized behaviors.
- Physical trauma can associate pleasure or approval with pain, failure to appreciate pain in others, or overreaction to perceived abuse
- Symptoms might include flashbacks, anxiety attacks, bizarre behaviors, abnormal eating patterns, poor sleep, nightmares, overreaction to minor related stimuli (triggers), physical pain in areas that were injured in abuse even when there is no physical reason, stomach pain, headaches, overreaction to minor physical symptoms, unusual fears, or avoidance.

Triggers

Triggers are stimuli of some sort that provoke a memory or feeling related to the experienced trauma. It can be a sight, a sound, a type of touch, a particular smell (the same deodorant or cologne her uncle wore when he was abusing her, body odor, environmental smells particular to the area where trauma occurred), familiar situations or places, attitudes (reacting in a similar way as to someone associated with the trauma), certain words or expressions, types of punishment (abuse may have been physical and was associated with spanking to point of injury, so this type of punishment used again would be very likely to trigger), confinement (holding a raging child who now feels rape is happening all over again), hugs (could stimulate a pleasant sexual reaction or aversion, anxiety, and fear). There might be other stimuli, but the triggers can do the following:

- Activate memories
- Start flashbacks
- Instigate behaviors
- Promote panic or bizarre behaviors
- Cause nightmares

Flashbacks

- This is the experience of reliving or re-experiencing, often in vivid detail, a particular traumatic memory.
- Flashbacks often are associated with feelings of fear or terror and autonomic arousal.
- They are often associated with a particular trigger.
- They can result in dissociation or bizarre behaviors.
- As a result of the flashbacks, the child might experience hallucinations— visual, tactile (touching), auditory, or even smells (olfactory), or complex audiovisual reenactments of the traumatic event.

Dissociation

- If, during the course of particularly brutal trauma, one submits to a self-hypnotic state and effectively leaves the situation, this is a dissociative defense. No conscious memory for that particular event occurs.

- Later in life, when no longer needed, the hypnotic states might recur—this is called *dissociation.*
- In severe cases, new personalities might develop. This is known as dissociative identity disorder or multiple personality disorder. This can occur with children and is much easier treated when younger than as an adult.

Physiologic and Behavioral Responses

Flashbacks or triggers might result in the following:

- Increased blood pressure
- Sweating
- Increased heart rate
- Panic attacks
- Sudden impulses to cut on self or injure others
- Suicidal behaviors
- Rages, some dissociative, in which the child does not recall what happened prior to or during the rage

Approaches in the Home

To provide the proper approaches for the traumatized child, it is necessary to know a bit more about the child than just the name and where he or she came from. We need to learn the basic story of each child. See chapter 9.

It is necessary to know not necessarily the grim details of the trauma but basic information:

- Type of Trauma: How would you classify the trauma? Sexual, physical, grief and loss, witness of trauma, disruption of relationships, abandonment, emotional abuse?
- How Long: What was the duration approximately? More than once? Repeated over months or years?
- How Severe: See above for examples of mild, moderate, severe.
- Possible Triggers: Have staffers already noted some special triggers or reactions? Does the child know what might be a trigger?
- History of Flashbacks: If present, of what do they consist? What type of hallucination? What helps to calm the child?

- History of Dissociation: Does the child have times he or she does not recall what he or she was doing, or seem to have moments of confusion or disorientation? Is there rage with the dissociation?
- Boundaries: Are there problems with proper respect of interpersonal boundaries? If so, there might be a need for closer vigilance.
- Sexualized Children: Confusion of boundaries is often taught by the abuse. Special consideration as noted later is very important. (See chapter 11, Sexual Abuse and Sexualized Children.)
- Physically Abused Children: Does the child confuse acceptance with physical pain or degrading comments? Sometimes, when a child has not known anything but violence, love was not demonstrated to her. Acceptance by the ones who should have loved and cared for her is replaced by abuse, physical pain, demeaning words. Now in a positive environment and treated with love and respect, the child can be confused about what it means. Why are you not hitting me? Why are you being nice? The sense of self has been so distorted as to feel that acceptance is abuse.

Reminder:

The Role of Caregiver Is to Do the Following:

- Provide structure.
- Be a listening ear.
- Provide encouragement, correction, direction.
- Assure that basic needs are met in a timely fashion.
- Be a mentor and example.
- Maintain appropriate boundaries.

The Role of Caregiver Is Not These Things:

- Rescuer
- Intimate confidant
- Therapist
- Doctor

Transference and Countertransference

It is important to understand the basics of this concept. Our past affects us, and the child's past affects him or her. We might react based on our past and what the child represents in us, as well as the child reacting to the caregiver due to the caregiver coming to represent something in the child's past. The representations might actually be good sometimes, but are often negative. However, if properly understood, even the negative can serve to promote healing.

- Transference: Transferring to the therapist or caregiver attributes of an important individual in the child's past.
- Countertransference: The caregiver or therapist transferring attributes of someone important in his or her own past onto the child.

Transference

- The child may see you as the hated mother who abandoned him in the past and react to you in a hateful way.
- This might result in verbal and physical aggression and difficulty forming a relationship until it is worked through.
- The child might see in a male caregiver representation of an abuser from the past and react to the person in that way.

Countertransference

- You might see in the child something from your past that causes you to react from the subconscious in a way that is not beneficial to the child. For example, the child might speak or act in a manner that is reflective of your mother or father with whom you had a conflicted relationship.

Knowing yourself and your own vulnerabilities is a first step in being able to react appropriately in these situations. Knowing the child and his or her history is helpful in understanding reactions and dealing with them. Of note, as attachment proceeds, the intensity of these reactions can increase due to the question the child has in his own mind about trusting the caregiver enough to attach. Maybe he might be concerned that you will be like all the others and that he will be bitterly disappointed yet again. It is your job to gradually show him that you're trustworthy and loving and that he is safe to make an attachment and work through the sometimes terrible memories.

Therapeutic Approaches

It is clearly not the role of the caregiver to be the therapist, but it is very helpful to understand the various approaches used to properly and compassionately deal with the traumatized child. If symptoms are persistent and not responsive to what you are doing in the home, then a qualified therapist/counselor would usually be the first approach, but with severe symptoms, a psychiatric provider needs to be the first option.

Medication Approaches

The goal of medication is to treat symptoms that are interfering with the life and development of the child so that the child can get back on the proper developmental track. Many symptoms respond to approaches by the caregiver, some in counseling, but the more difficult symptoms often need intervention of psychiatric medications. Often, if the symptoms are severe, therapeutic approaches are not possible until the distress is relieved.

Symptoms that are able to be helped with medication approaches include:

- Depression
- Anxiety
- Flashbacks
- Mood swings
- Rage
- Sleep disorders: nightmares, sleepwalking, behaviors during dreams (REM behaviors), insomnia, night terrors.
- Panic attacks
- Dissociation

Therapy Approaches:

Medications will help in the short-term and often allow the therapy to proceed. The goal of therapy is to resolve the symptoms to the best degree possible to allow attachment and development to proceed.

- Cognitive Behavioral Techniques: This type of therapy is to help the client to deal with misperceptions and cognitive distortions helping to provide a way the client is able to properly perceive what is going on in their lives, to see themselves in a more realistic way, and to be able to persistently tell themselves the truth.
- EMDR: Eye Movement Desensitization and Reprocessing. This is a technique that has several decades of effective use. It is based on an assumption that you need to connect both sides of the brain while processing the trauma by alternatively tapping one leg and then the other or moving eyes from side to side. The therapist can help the client to safely process the trauma, learn techniques of putting the trauma away when not discussing it in the session, and eventually coming to the point that the memories and flashbacks are no longer controlling the individual.
- Traditional Counseling: This involves slowly exploring what needs to be explored of the trauma in the past and connecting it to what is happening in current time. It involves supportive techniques which help strengthen a person's defense mechanisms (how you deal with stress and life). Expressive techniques are also used including art and music to assist with identifying feelings and working on ways to deal with what happened in a more balanced way. There is also psycho-education which involves helping the client to understand their disorder and what happened to them.
- Other Approaches: There are many forms of therapy and many are effective but mostly fall into the above categories. Counseling/therapy is effective and helpful.
- Precautions: It is very important that the counselor understands and has experience working with trauma. Sometimes, when dealing with these very difficult memories, there is a phenomenon called Flooding. This can be very dangerous as the client is flooded with memories, feelings, flashbacks resulting in severe anxiety and sometimes self-destructive behaviors. If this is occurring after sessions, the counselor needs to know and the caregiver needs to monitor the child for suicidal/self-destructive behaviors and respond accordingly to keep the child safe. After sessions, it is important to assess how the child is responding. There may be some difficult behaviors, anger immediately following a difficult session. This is self-protection. They might need some time alone or time to talk afterward. It is important as a caregiver to be understanding about this.

In Summary

To help the child, consider these approaches:

- Seek to understand the child in context, knowing his or her *story.*
- Learn what the patterns of reactions are and what might be the triggers.
- Learn to avoid triggers as much as possible.
- Avoid discussing the trauma with the child. If he or she discloses, listen but do not encourage further disclosure. This needs to be managed by a professional counselor or doctor if such is available to you.
- Use compassionate understanding in the context of established boundaries and structure. This basically means to stop and think about what you are doing.
- Use approaches that do not cause triggering and provide an environment in which he or she can feel safe and where harm will not befall him or her.
- Understand the unique character of each child and learn how to address his or her special needs.
- Be flexible and creative in your caregiving style.
- Make use of counseling and psychiatric care when available.

Debbie was age nine when she arrived at the children's home in the United States. She was born in China and lived there until she was three or four, when she was adopted. From what she could remember, she underwent serious abuse while in the Chinese orphanage. Arriving at her adoptive home, she did not connect with her adoptive parents. Normal attachment did not proceed. She developed severe and self-destructive behaviors. She came to the point that her parents could no longer care for her. She had conflicted with her mother to the point where her mother could not stand to be around her. She was sent to the children's home at that point. After she was left off at the children's home, her parents traveled back to the state where they lived. On arrival, they called back and said they were finished, that they never wanted to see Debbie again. Do not have her call or write. In one of the more difficult emotional sessions in my thirty years of work with children, the director and I had to sit down with the child and explain that her parents no longer wanted her. It was very difficult. Through the next year, her anger was rather intense. She did finally engage in some therapy and was started on medication to help with some trauma-related symptoms. During some of the years, she was on a good deal of medication just to keep her safe. She started to calm down enough eventually to begin to attach to staff members. During her teen years, she was again rather difficult but gradually grew into a loving, mature Christian adult. She has dedicated her life to working with children in care and is quite knowledgeable about trauma and attachment problems!

Notes

11

Sexual Abuse and Sexualized Children

Sexual trauma unfortunately seems to be on the increase among children coming into care. Often, caregivers are rather shocked at what they see or hear from the children. These children need some special attention and understanding, and the caregiver needs to be prepared with some understanding and tools to be able to help them through this and allow them to develop normally. For some, it may be quite a challenge to love these children when their behavior so offends us.

Review of Attachment

To properly understand the effect of sexual trauma, take some time to review the stages of attachment. This helps you see what the effect of trauma might be during development.

- In order to properly psychologically develop, each child must successfully complete all stages of attachment.

- Failure of or incomplete attachment is known as *reactive attachment disorder* and leads to all manner of problems.
- Interference from trauma can disrupt the attachment process.

Sexual Development

One way to more easily understand development and the brain is by the concept of layering. Each phase of development provides another level or layer of complexity. What is likely happening is that the brain develops more tracts or wiring to connect different parts of the brain with other parts. When sexual development is completed properly and in the right sequence, the person is able to deal properly with sexual feelings and sexual identity. If not accomplished properly, things tend to go wrong.

- Sexual development starts at birth during initial bonding with the mother.
- The next layer is attachment at around eight months.
- The next layer is separation individuation at eighteen months to three years. This now sets the pattern for future relationships. First, there is the bonding, then attachment (special closeness), then pulling back to a healthier give-and-take relationship.

Age three to six

- There is some self-exploration and noting of differences of the opposite-sex sibling if one is present. There also can be the discovery that exploring the genitals causes some pleasure response.
- The child continues now with peer relationships forming, best friend generally the same sex, and there is a gradual deepening of significant relationships. Approximating (drawing close) and distancing (pulling away) occurs as in primary attachment. Each relationship is based on the foundation of the initial attachment with the primary caregiver. Some relationships go through the attachment process and endure while others fall away.

Age six to eleven

- Relationships progress, some playing "house" or "doctor," show-and-tell.
- There is a natural curiosity of the opposite sex.

- The child is not ready for any detailed sexual information.

Age eleven to thirteen

- The child starts developing an interest in the opposite sex but still prefers same-sex relationships.
- Self-exploration might result in masturbation, mostly males, some females.
- At this point, the child is very vulnerable to sexual information and ready to engage in appropriate dialogue. This is a good time to start appropriate sexual education before they learn too much from their peers.

Age thirteen to sixteen

- The child develops group relationships with the opposite sex, socializing together with males and females, but is not ready emotionally or physically for a one-on-one relationship.
- At this time, there is a high vulnerability to sexual stimulation of any type, which can easily draw a child into inappropriate behavior which can develop into an established pattern.

Ages sixteen to nineteen

- There is development of one-on-one opposite-sex relationships, and the child can tolerate some sexual stimulation.
- Relationships can be tolerated that are very close, more emotionally ready than at age thirteen.

Age seventeen and above

- Now with all the layers of development in place, the young person is able to tolerate the sexual stimulation of a marital relationship without harm and in a healthy manner.
- Sexual stimulation prior to the brain being ready tends to short-circuit developing tracts, causing abnormal responses and confusion.
- Sexual stimulation with all the layers and tracts developed is wholesome, tolerable, and healthy.

Developmental Vulnerability

- As with any other trauma, sexual trauma is more likely to cause lasting damage during periods of developmental vulnerability.

Sexual Trauma

The effect of sexual trauma as noted in the prior chapter has to be considered in the context of the victim, environment, and the type and intensity of the trauma. You can review the considerations for mild, moderate, and severe trauma in chapter 10, Understanding Childhood Trauma.

- Effect of trauma is a combination of duration, severity, and intensity of trauma on a vulnerable or resilient child who may or may not have family support or social supports.
- Is child already a vulnerable child, suffering attachment disorder, mental disorder, or lack of family support?
- Has the child previously endured sexual trauma?
- Did the support system believe the disclosure of the trauma?
- Has the trauma led to symptom development or abnormal behaviors?
- Has the child begun to sexually victimize others?

Symptoms and Behaviors

- The type of symptoms or behavior is highly dependent on the developmental stage, vulnerability, and intensity and severity of trauma.
- Symptoms can be severe to the point of being very difficult to manage even in residential care.
- Sexual stimulation prior to the brain's readiness to adapt to the stimuli will short-circuit the sexual response, causing confusion, and can result in specific sexualized behaviors.
- There also might be sleep disturbance, nightmares, or night terrors.
- Similar to other trauma, there can be anxiety, exaggerated startle response, avoidance of trauma-related activities or places, or triggers that produce the symptoms or behaviors.

- Flashbacks—visual, auditory, sensory, tactile—can include unwanted sexual arousal.
- Dissociation, with or without alternative personality development, can occur.
- Sexualized behaviors might include disrobing, attempting to disrobe others, touching others, masturbation in any given situation, attempting to kiss or fondle others including caregivers, lying on top or encouraging others to lie on top of him or her, or other imitative behaviors of the sexual act.
- Sexualized behaviors also include sexual talk, use of vulgar terms in public, seductive language with others including adults, grooming behaviors, such as preparing another child to become a victim.

Confusion of emotions due to paired associations might occur:

- **Affection and sexual arousal.** As the child develops close personal relationships, the closeness and affection might produce actual sexual excitation not under the child's voluntary control, as the brain has connected the two, due to the short circuit.
- **Anger and sexual arousal.** If there was abuse that included degradation and anger, there might be a pairing of anger and sexual arousal. This might lead the child to try to make the caregivers or other children angry just to get the feeling.
- **Violence and sexual arousal.** This pairing is very distressing and, if not addressed early, could lead to seriously dangerous behaviors. There also might be triggers for sexual arousal in watching violent movies or playing games that include some form of violence.
- **Sexual arousal and guilt, emotional pain, fear, terror.** In this case, the arousal that might be normal in later adolescence results in aversion of close relationships as it brings painful memories.
- **Sexual arousal and physical pain.** If not properly dealt with, the child might later develop aberrant sexual practices, which involve the pairing of pain and pleasure. This would include sadism, masochism, fetishism, and so forth. These children might also be more likely to self-injure as not only is there the normal numbing response that occurs with self-injury, there might be more of a pleasure response. This would result from abuse that was very painful but arousing at the same time.

Self-Injurious Behaviors

- Scratching, cutting, hitting self, putting self in dangerous situations
- Erasing self, using pencil erasers to cause self-injury
- Head banging (this may be caused by other conditions as well)
- Suicidal behaviors
- Masturbation to the point of causing physical damage
- Bulimic or anorexic symptoms
  - *Bulimia* in children can be represented by binge eating to the point of abdominal pain, then inducing vomiting to relieve the pain; the process causes numbness like self-cutting.
  - *Anorexia* is the avoidance of intake of food, although one might be obsessively interested in the preparation. The avoidance results in dangerous weight loss, girls' menstruation cycles might stop, and other health concerns may develop from the poor nutrition. This behavior sometimes is associated with a desire to not grow up and to not become a sexual being.

Spiritual Concerns

- Sex is considered a sacred act.
- Sex joins a married couple, causing them to become one, in the same way joining those who are not married.
- Sex outside God's boundaries results in spiritual sickness.
- Trauma links (the connection between the victim and the perpetrator) might include spiritual concerns and must be considered in the treatment.

Treatment Approaches

- Removal of any and all sexually stimulating material from environment.
- Structure to include close observation and knowledge of sexual predilection of the child.
- Exploration of any spiritual concerns and following of the guidelines mentioned later in the manual (see chapter 17).
- Corrective attachment approaches, maintaining the structure and vigilance necessary to allow normal development.

- Reasonable reaction to the sexual behaviors, treating them in a calm but firm redirection or appropriate consequence, understanding that much of this is not under the child's awareness or control, even if we feel totally disgusted.
- Working with the child on establishing and respecting boundaries, reinforcing along the way as necessary.
- Be very alert for sneaky behaviors that can develop.
- Not engaging in a battle if you somehow discover that the child is sexually mature and masturbates in private and is not in excess (not causing more behaviors or distractions).
- Addressing masturbation behavior if it is excessive, in public, or causing distress for others in the home, or producing more sexual behaviors.
- Counseling, which can be helpful if it does not excessively explore the past trauma but does more to work with the here and now, what is going on in the child's current life situation, its relation to the past, and how to control the impulses and be more appropriate in their behavior. EMDR as mentioned in prior chapter may be helpful.
- Working through the Seven Steps to Freedom in Christ, as the child becomes old enough to complete them, as outlined in Neil Anderson's books: The Bondage Breaker series (see reference list).

Medication might be useful to reduce distress in some instances:

- To allow attachment to proceed
- Target self-injurious behaviors
- Relieve depression
- Reduce flashbacks, sexual behaviors, anxiety, sleep disturbance

The goal of medication treatment is to act as a bridge, not a permanent solution, to relieve the distressing behaviors sufficiently so that counseling can then be effective and the child can return to his developmental track. Generally, the medication can be discontinued once attachment has proceeded and counseling is making progress unless there is an underlying chronic mental illness.

Notes

12

Sexuality Education in the Home

In the normal Christian home, it is the parents' job to provide sexuality education for their preadolescent children. As the world is the main teacher of this topic, our children are bombarded with false and misleading information with no moral foundation. It is, therefore, even more vital that our orphans be provided the correct information and the opportunity to decide to live sexually pure lives. The ages at which this information can be best learned and not provoke problems are around age eleven for girls and age twelve for boys. This is around the time the body is just beginning to change for both. For those having suffered sexual abuse, some education needs to be provided along the way but mostly boundaries, redirecting inappropriate behaviors, proper touch, and so forth.

The manner in which the information can be provided varies but should roughly follow the outline provided here so as to cover all the important aspects. It can be done in five sections, which will be further elaborated to allow your own development of the appropriate curriculum.

The sessions need to be constructed in such a way that the same-sex caregivers are involved. It might require the help of a counselor or medical professional to explain the first two part especially. It can be done in a retreat format, completing all of the lessons in one evening or overnight. Alternatively, there could be several sessions lasting for one to two hours each night for five nights. These are the topics to discuss:

1. Anatomy and the Developing Body
2. The Sexual Act
3. Sex and the Bible
4. Consequences of Disobedience
5. Commitment to Sexual Purity

1. Anatomy and the Developing Body

This section needs to include some diagrams and drawings that can be obtained from the Internet or other sources. The diagrams should show the process of physical development and what changes occur through puberty. The proper names for each part of the anatomy must be provided, which will help correct those who know the common vulgar terms.

For the girls, spend a bit more time explaining menses and what is happening to their bodies each month. Allow them to feel comfortable enough to ask questions. The boys will not need quite as many details regarding menstruation (such as feminine hygiene) but do need to understand the process.

Once the anatomy is explained along with the changes that are happening to their bodies, have a few words about modesty and physical boundaries, as well as appropriate and inappropriate touch.

2. The Sexual Act

So as not to produce arousal but to explain things in a matter-of-fact way, this session can be rather short and to the point. The vocabulary needed includes arousal, ejaculation, and orgasm. A short explanation and brief description of each is sufficient. After that is done, follow the sperm to the egg with the help of diagrams to explain what happens to produce the new life. Talk at this point needs to include that as soon as the sperm makes it into the ova, the new life is a person and will become an adult someday if all goes well. Briefly trace the development of the baby in the context of the wonderful complexities of God's new creation. Whenever possible, remind the children of the spiritual aspects of a loving sexual relationship.

3. Sex and the Bible

This section can be very interesting and fun, as well as informative. One way to do it is a "Sword Drill." Everyone brings a Bible to class. Verses are assigned to each one to read and make a short commentary. (The verses can be found in any Bible; many have indexes or concordances. Other references can be useful, such as *Nave's Topical Bible.*) The instructor will cover topics of marriage, lust, adultery, fornication, and other areas that are pertinent, being sure to cover important passages such as those that address issues concerning married life found in 1 Corinthians 7.

4. Consequences to Disobedience

This is another section that could benefit from the input of a health professional. The consequences of sex outside of marriage need to be discussed, including the possibility of pregnancy, AIDS, other sexually transmitted diseases, and psychological consequences (adultery, marital breakup, consequences of sex before marriage). The facts need to be presented clearly and concisely, so there is understanding that there is danger outside of God's plan.

5. Commitment to Sexual Purity

After all is said and done, participants can take time to consider the benefits of following God's direction, understanding His plan for sexuality in the context of a healthy God-centered marriage. Some parents incorporate a special dedication prayer, some invite children to sign special pledges, some even have cards made with the promise and a place for a signature. Others have found that the use of symbolic jewelry commemorating the pledge makes it meaningful—a necklace for the girls with a designed key, for example. This key can be presented to the husband on the wedding night, symbolizing the sharing of their love together. Nowadays, the boys might even like something similar or possibly a bracelet.

Notes

13

Preparation for Independent Living

Preparing to leave home and accept responsibility for your own upkeep requires a number of skills that are normally acquired in a typical family home to the point that at about eighteen to twenty-one years of age, one is ready to launch. Some are more ready than others in a normal home. The nice thing in a normal family is that you have support as you go out. When children are leaving an out-of-home placement situation, it is a different story. It is important that the process be started during the teen years, with both the adolescent and the caregiver working together through the list of skills that need to be established so a successful transition occurs. This can be exciting yet filled with anxiety. Some kids do not want to leave, due to fear of failure on their own. Being sure the child is prepared can be assisted with the following protocol, which can also help reduce some of the anxiety.

1. Getting Ready to Go

- Understands attachment and grief process
- Able to leave in a good way, maintaining relationship with caregivers and friends
- Is capable of changing status of relationships but not cutting them off
- Able to adjust to life away from home

As the adolescent is now facing departure soon, he or she needs to become aware of how it will feel to make the transition. He or she will go through grief and want to just leave and not look back. Now that the teen has learned to connect with others and to value relationships, he or she will be guided in how to transition in a safe and healthy way, maintaining relationships where possible. This involves being ready to invest time and energy to preserve important relations.

2. Health and Personal Hygiene

- Daily self-care, showering, brushing teeth, use of deodorant, shaving
- Understanding of normal bodily functions
- Knows when to seek medical help
- First-aid knowledge
- Proper exercise

Now that the adolescent faces being on his or her own, it would be easy to stop doing those things that were rather forced when first arrived. Over time, we need to provide bits of information as to why these activities are important to maintain health and avoid unnecessary discomfort.

3. Nutrition

- A balanced diet
- Buying groceries within a budget
- Preparing and storing food, including basic cooking skills

It can be helpful to gradually start using the children in the kitchen and when shopping so that the skills can be demonstrated. Short talks about food, sharing what is healthy and what is not, can be helpful. Spending time helping to prepare food, learning how to operate the machines in the kitchen, knowing what needs to be refrigerated and what an expiration date means. It is also important to teach the child how to read the labels on the purchased food items and what makes food healthy or not so healthy.

4. Care for Clothing

- Buying adequate clothing
- Proper washing, drying, folding, storing
- Dressing appropriately for climate, job, conditions, etc.

Many of the above tasks are often managed by facility staff if child resides in a large orphanage or childcare facility; if child is a young teen, he/she can be included in caring for the laundry and having regular chores related to this. Shopping for clothes within one's budget is very important to understand as well as what type of clothes does one need for particular jobs and so forth.

5. Money and Finances

- Understanding the financial system
- Bank accounts and use of checks, credit cards, and keeping track of money
- Proper basic budgeting skills

This part is a bit more difficult to address, as many homes do not have the funds to provide allowances. However, most can encourage the older teens to look for part-time employment. When money is earned, counsel can be provided as to what the money means and how to properly use it, how to budget and how to manage an account, use of credit cards and the newer technology. It is a bit more difficult now in a digital society that often the money is just numbers going from your account to the account of the store. It is even more important to learn to read the statement from the bank and keep track of what is spent.

6. Taking Care of Your Home

- Appliances
- Care of the kitchen
- Carpet and floor care
- Bathroom care

- Bedroom care, including making the bed
- Laundry care
- Outdoor maintenance, caring for yard, landscaping, keeping space clean

Taking care of your own place will have hopefully been demonstrated by staff in the home. Having in mind that the child is going to grow up and is going to need to know a lot of things can help to guide you in providing opportunities to see how things are done. Finding those teachable moments throughout the day to show how things are done are very important.

7. Transportation

- Public transportation, how to use it
- Purchasing and maintaining a vehicle
- Appropriate driving skills and licensing (car and driver)

The type of transportation skills needed vary widely with the location of the home and what is available economically and practically. For some, managing a bicycle in traffic may be all that is needed, along with some idea how to use public transport. In US culture, it is generally necessary to provide driver training and associated skills as well as how to care for the car.

8. Spiritual Skills

- Daily time with God, Bible reading, and prayer
- Finding a church
- Developing good spiritual habits

If regular devotional time was not observed as part of the structure of the home, then there will be major deficits in this area, and the likelihood of a child continuing attendance of church and serving the Lord is rather low. This skill is demonstrated and picked up as it is part of the external structure that becomes internalized.

9. Leisure Skills

- Wisely using time without overspending
- Developing healthy habits of exercise and hobbies
- Keeping up the sporting skills developed in the growing-up years

During the growing-up years, part of the process is to have fun together. Promoting friendly competition and enjoyable times creates memories so that when we are grown, we want to do the same for our families. Do not forget the importance of sports for those who can participate, as well as other ways to have fun so that the children leave with a good idea on what is a balanced life.

10. Job-Related Skills

- Looking for work, internships, or apprenticeships
- Interviewing, writing a resumé, filling out applications
- Obtaining and maintaining employment
- Advancing in the job

It is important to have some connections in the community, especially for the orphanage type care-model, but also for the adoption/foster care model, to be able to have some part-time jobs for the older teens to engage in and to learn how to work, how to get along with the coworkers and boss. If there is a relationship with the businesses, the caregiver or administrative staff can assist with any problems that might arise.

11. Educational Skills

- Setting and reaching goals
- Study skills
- Self-discipline
- Surviving and thriving in the university or technical-school environment

As the child starts out in the home, hopefully he or she will see that education is very important by the emphasis on learning promoted by the staff. As education is promoted, we need to take care with those who do not seem to be able to learn as well and to provide special help or seek out testing to see if the child is capable of progressing with education.

Expectations need to be reality based. Those who really cannot progress with school need to be helped to find other areas that they can succeed in.

12. Interpersonal Skills

- Choosing friends and maintaining friendships
- Resisting temptations
- Maintaining appropriate interpersonal boundaries

With successful corrective attachment, interpersonal relationships should start to become less problematic. However, skills in this area are often lacking. The adolescent may need some extra help with how to make and keep friends, especially those just starting into the teen years so that they can have strong relationships when it is time to leave the home and they will be able to continue to make and keep friends.

13 Dating and Relationships with the Opposite Sex

- Development of appropriate understanding of proper dating behavior and safety
- Proper moral understanding
- Respect for the opposite sex

Open dialogue during the late teen years is vital to be able to help these skills develop and allow safe relationships to develop. As questions come up, be ready to address them. There will be heartbreaks and difficulties in every teen's life, but these normal events are often not well tolerated in those who are a bit fragile in their connections.

14. Problem-Solving Skills

- Analyzing a problem
- Previewing the possible scenarios and solutions
- Formulating a plan
- Checking results

As problems come up, don't just provide a solution, but instead, use it as a teachable moment and work on teaching the skill of previewing, which is often missing with RAD children as well as those with ADHD. This is a process of imagining or predicting what will or may happen if I make this decision instead of that one. Interesting discussions can proceed during a time of conversation by providing an imaginary crisis and finding out how the teens might resolve the situation.

Use the above outline to develop some lessons or devotions to assist in promoting the idea that one day, the child will leave the home and you want him to be ready for the challenge. It can also serve as a guide to the caregiver to assign chores or responsibilities gradually, as the child is growing so as to acquire many of the needed skills.

You also might want to use it like a checklist that the teen can keep in her room to check off those things she has accomplished or feels comfortable with. See the next page for a complete checklist, which can be copied for use with the children who are looking to launch in the next two or three years.

Independence Prep Checklist

1 GETTING READY TO GO

— Understands attachment and grief process
— Able to leave in a positive way, maintaining relationships with caregivers and friends
— Capable of changing status of relationships but not cutting them off
— Able to adjust to life away from home

2. HEALTH AND PERSONAL HYGIENE

— Demonstrates ability to engage in daily self-care, showering, brushing teeth, use of deodorant, shaving
— Able to understand normal bodily functions
— Knows when to seek medical help
— Has basic first-aid knowledge
— Able to obtain proper exercise

3. NUTRITION

— Understands what is a balanced diet
— Knows how to buy groceries within a budget
— Understands basics of food storage, what to freeze, what to refrigerate
— Has basic cooking skills and can prepare meals

4. CARE OF CLOTHING

— Knows how to buy adequate clothing
— Demonstrates knowledge of how to care for clothing: washing, drying, folding
— Knows proper storage of clothing, keeping dirty clothes in one place and clean in another
— Able to dress appropriately for climate, job, conditions, and situations

5. MONEY AND FINANCES

— Has basic understanding of the financial system
— Demonstrates basic understanding of banking account, credit cards, including appropriate usage and how to pay bills
— Has adequate understanding of proper basic budgeting skills

6. TAKING CARE OF YOUR HOME

— Understands how to operate and care for appliances
— Demonstrates adequate care and cleaning of the kitchen, dishes, utensils, pots, and pans
— Knows basic carpet and floor care
— Able to care for, clean, and maintain the bathroom
— Knows basic bedroom care, including making the bed, washing the bedclothes
— Has adequate skills for outdoor maintenance, caring for yard, landscaping, keeping space clean

7. TRANSPORTATION

— Understands public transportation and how to use it
— Has adequate knowledge of purchasing and maintaining a vehicle
— Demonstrates appropriate driving skills and licensing (car and driver)

8. SPIRITUAL SKILLS

— Has habit of spending daily time with God, Bible reading, and prayer
— Knows how to find a church
— Is developing good spiritual habits

9. LEISURE SKILLS

— Can understand how to wisely use time without overspending
— Is developing healthy habits of exercise and hobbies
— Has plans to keep up the sporting skills developed in the growing-up years

10. JOB-RELATED SKILLS

— Knows basics of job searching
— Knows basics of how to interview, write a resumé, and fill out applications
— Is capable of obtaining and maintaining employment
— Has understanding about advancing in the job, doing well at assigned duties

11. EDUCATIONAL SKILLS (if planning to further education)

— Is able to set goals and work to reach them
— Has basic study skills
— Self-discipline is demonstrated
— Has capacity to be able to survive and thrive in the university or technical-school environment

12. INTERPERSONAL SKILLS

— Has skills in choosing friends and maintaining friendships
— Is becoming good at resisting temptations
— Has a sense of how to maintain appropriate interpersonal boundaries

13. DATING AND RELATIONSHIPS WITH THE OPPOSITE SEX

— Has developed an appropriate understanding of proper dating behavior and safety
— Has proper moral understanding
— Has developed proper respect for the opposite sex

14. PROBLEM-SOLVING SKILLS

— Is able to analyze a problem
— Has ability to preview possible scenarios and solutions
— Can formulate a plan
— Is able to critically check results and make changes as necessary

Notes

14

Understanding Mental Illness in Children

Praise be to the God and Father of our Lord Jesus Christ, the Father of compassion and the God of all comfort, who comforts us in all our troubles, so that we can comfort those in any trouble with the comfort we ourselves receive from God.
—2 Corinthians 1:3–4

Children who come into care might suffer from any one of a number of mental disorders. There are quite a few, but the main ones fall into just three categories. The fact that the child suffers from a mental illness should not necessarily of itself inform the decision to accept or not accept into care. However, if there is evidence of a severe persistent disorder and there is not available psychiatric care, it might be wise to have the child placed where such care can be provided. The illnesses can be minor, not really requiring much other than supportive care, or serious in which medications are necessary to preserve the life of the child. What follows is a general outline. The actual list of possible disorders is much longer. This is meant as a guide so proper referral can be made, if needed, to a mental-health professional.

Categories

- Anxiety disorders
- Mood disorders
- Psychotic disorders

Basic Principles

- Adjustment disorders, situational stress, transient anxiety, and depression, not biologically based: These can generally be addressed with supportive care and, if available, some short-term counseling.
- Mental illness and developmental syndromes are biological and based on brain chemistry or anatomic abnormalities: these very often have to be addressed "biologically"—that is, with medication approaches as part of the treatment.

Assessment and Treatment Guidelines

- Approach is holistic: bio-psycho-socio-spiritual
- Assessment and treatment must look at the whole picture

As the disorder is assessed, it is necessary to incorporate the ***biological*** factors of the illness, which are the chemical or structural problems in the brain. The ***psychological*** factors are those that have to do with the child's sense of self or belonging—self-im-age, self-esteem, sense of identity, security, and vulnerability. The ***socio*** factors have to do with attachment, connection to peers, caregivers, others in the community, cultural connections. The ***spiritual*** factors apply to assessing the spiritual impact of the disorder—how it affects one's relationship with God and how sin might be involved or evil influence might be a part of the picture. Similarly, with treatment, we need to address all four factors, some more than others. Sometimes, taking care of the biological or spiritual issues, when these factors are dominant and the child responds well to the treatment, can help bring the other factors in line.

Treatment has the goal of placing the child back on track developmentally when possible. If the illness is severe and the child cannot be brought back to normal developmental stages, then we do all that is possible to enhance the child's quality of life.

Anxiety Disorders

- Generalized Anxiety: This is a state of increased reactivity to the environment, physiologic reactions to minor stressors, fear, worry.
- Panic Disorder: It is characterized by discrete episodes of severe anxiety, lasting several minutes to hours, associated with heightened arousal. Symptoms might include sweating, fast heartbeat, a sense of doom, and abdominal or chest pain. Anxiety might be so severe as to trigger impulsive and self-destructive behaviors that can endanger the child's life. It might be associated with a trauma trigger, which needs to be explored with the child and addressed as discussed in the information on trauma. See chapter 10.

Obsessive-Compulsive Disorder (OCD)

- Obsessions: This involves recurrent unwanted thoughts.
- Compulsions: This applies to recurrent unwanted actions often in response to, or to reduce, obsessions. It might manifest itself as compulsive hand washing due to a fear of germs (obsessions about germs), writing and rewriting (never satisfied with how it looks), counting objects, ritualistic behaviors such as superstitions, but taking them very seriously, evening out, straightening, repetitive behaviors due to not getting it quite right (just-right compulsions). This could be something like having to go through the door several times before finally entering a room.

Mood Disorder

- ***Major Depression*:** This consists of one or more episodes of depressed mood, low energy, irritability, sadness, and thoughts of running away or suicide. It can also include loss of or increased appetite and increased or decreased sleep. It can be associated with psychotic symptoms (loss of reality orientation), but in children, that usually means bipolar (see below).
- ***Bipolar II Disorder***: Along with depression, this person has had at least one episode of hypomania (a state of increased energy), intrusiveness, increased goal-directed behavior, impulsivity, and racing thoughts, but not to the level of mania in which one is likely to lose control and become disorganized. This bipolar disorder is not associated with psychosis. It is best described as little ups and big downs.

- ***Bipolar I Disorder*:** This is characterized by at least one episode of mania, very high energy states, decreased need for sleep, increased goal-directed behavior, scattered thoughts, impulsivity, excessive pleasure seeking, possible disorganization, and psychotic symptoms. There may or may not be an associated depressive episode, which often follows a manic high.
- ***Bipolar Mixed*:** These patients have cycles of mania and depression that might occur during the course of a day or have manic and depressive symptoms simultaneously. This might be described as a high-energy depression and can be associated with psychosis. There is a higher potential for suicide than I or II. Most children fit in this category, as episodes are short and swings can be rapid. It can easily be confused with ADHD since many of the symptoms are the same. However, bipolar is an episodic or cyclic disorder— symptoms typically are not consistent over time.

Psychotic Disorders

- Delusions: fixed false beliefs that defy logic, reason, or contradictory facts
- Paranoia: suspiciousness of others, fearing harm to self or others, deriving negative or personal messages from otherwise neutral interactions or input, misinterpreting the intent of others, finding meaning in otherwise unimportant input; results in lack of trust, making the attachment process much more difficult
- Hallucinations: abnormal sensory experience unrelated to external stimuli
- Visual: *complex*—sees human or animal figures with or without audio; *simple*—sees colors shapes, amorphous objects
- Auditory: *complex*—hears a voice or voices with understandable output, can be commands or commentary; *simple*—hears just a noise, might be hard to define
- Tactile: a sense that one is being touched, hit, cut, etc.
- Gustatory: unstimulated sense of what is usually a foul taste
- Olfactory: unstimulated odor, usually very disgusting

Schizophrenia

A chronic disabling psychotic illness, it causes the patient to suffer from delusions, hallucinations, disordered thinking, language disturbance, and a sense of being controlled by external forces. The disorder is chronic and often progressive. If onset is during ages six to ten, the prognosis is grave, and the child will likely need long-term assistance.

Types of Schizophrenia

- Paranoid Type: predominantly paranoid or grandiose delusions, language is unimpaired generally
- Undifferentiated Type: might have paranoia, disturbance of language, mood instability, catatonia (becomes immobile, unresponsive, or hyperactive but unresponsive)
- Disorganized Type: occurs rarely, profound language disturbance, delusions are fragmented, severe hallucinations, hard to treat, often becomes demented
- Schizoaffective: often categorized on its own but with prominent schizophrenic-type symptoms with either mood swings, persistent depression, or persistent mania; might look like bipolar or depression, but the thought disorder (psychosis) persists and has symptoms like those of schizophrenia

Treatment

All of the above disorders are treated with various medications, which can relieve the symptoms and provide a better quality of life. Treatment with counseling can be helpful along with the medication. It might be harmful to not treat, as the symptoms might cause the child to become dangerous to self or others or render the sufferer gravely disabled, unable to care for himself, or to be able to discern reality.

Among the mental illnesses that may present in children, major depression would be the most common. It is very important that caregivers understand the symptoms and the risks of suicidal behavior. You may find it useful to have a depression rating scale to help assist with evaluating the child. This can also serve as information that can be provided to a physician or a mental-health professional.

To assist in evaluating the symptoms of depression, the Children's Depression Rating Scale (CDRS) can be downloaded free via Google or other search engines.

Notes

15

Developmental and Neuropsychiatric Disorders

The purpose of this section is to introduce you to some of the common disorders you might run into that are considered developmental or fall in the boundary between neurology and psychiatry. You are provided an outline of symptoms and presentations not for you to diagnose the children, but as a way to assist you in getting the needed help if you do find some of these symptoms present. It is very important to understand that these disorders may affect behavior and may be quite limiting to the child in his or her developmental experience as well as affect attachment. Arming yourself with a basic understanding can help you face the challenges that may present themselves.

Attention Deficit Hyperactivity Disorder (ADHD)

This lifelong persistent issue has the following characteristics:

- Inattention: problems with focusing, filtering, prioritizing input, and transferring input to active working and long-term memory
- Hyperactivity: increased level of random activity, not necessarily goal directed, high energy, difficulty sitting still
- Impulsivity: failure to stop and think prior to action, poor previewing skills
- Distractibility: attention is easily diverted to environmental stimuli as there is difficulty prioritizing input.

Autism Spectrum Disorder

A developmental disorder, diagnosed usually before age three, with many of the following characteristics:

- Deficits in reciprocal social interaction
- Poor nonverbal behaviors
- Poor or no peer interaction
- Little sharing of pleasure
- Lack of social and emotional reciprocity

Diagnostic Criteria

- Restricted, stereotypic, repetitive patterns of behaviors, interests, or activities
- Inflexible adherence to nonfunctional rituals or routines
- Lack of imaginative or symbolic play
- Preoccupation with parts of objects
- Seventy-five percent diagnosed as mentally retarded
- Fifteen percent to 30 percent with seizures
- Thirty-three percent with abnormal neurologic findings such as abnormal gait, toe walking
- Many with associated chromosomal abnormalities
- Many might have splinter skills (these are special areas in which the child operates at a normal or even above normal level despite overall functioning remaining low)

- Common traits include musical talents, ability to solve puzzles, memorizing, mimicking, mathematical calculating, ability to create perpetual calendars, hyperlexia (extremely good at reading despite other intellectual deficiencies), innate map-reading skills
- Often affectionate but lack common sense and judgment

Asperger's Syndrome

- First described in 1944 Austria by Dr. Hans Asperger
- A neurobiological disorder considered to be on the autistic spectrum
- Occurs in about one in 250 people (6:1 male-to-female ratio)

Description

- IQ is often in normal to superior range
- Impairments occur in sensorimotor, language, socialization, adaptive behavior, cognitive function areas
- They often have coexisting problems such as ADHD, anxiety disorders, depression, or bipolar disorder

Language impairment

- Pedantic or academic style, like the patient is teaching you
- Uses words or phrases repetitively
- Misunderstands subtleties, does not get subtle humor
- Literal in communication style
- Difficulty beginning, ending, or continuing conversations

Socialization

- Limited body language
- Limited eye contact, feelings of suspicion
- Problems relating to others
- Prefers adult company
- Few friends
- Does not respect personal space

- Lack of perspective taking (not able to see how others might feel or think in a given situation)

Maladaptive Behavior

- Does not always adapt behavior to situations
- Catastrophic reactions to minor changes, poor set shifting, difficult to change from one set of circumstances to another (stop playing and go eat dinner, for example)
- Engages in repetitive, obsessive, or ritualistic behavior
- Immature behaviors
- Problems controlling anger
- Frequently overwhelmed in demanding situations or crowds
- Attempts to impose routines or structures on others
- Difficulty regulating emotions, anger, aggression, and anxiety

Cognitive Aspects

- Superior ability in restricted areas of interest
- Obsessive interest in a narrow subject
- Does best with familiar or repeated tasks
- Excellent rote memory
- Learns best with pictures or written words
- Appears to be aware of his difference
- Lacks organization and common sense
- Difficulty understanding consequences to own behaviors

Sensorimotor

- Unusual reactions to loud or unpredictable noises
- Tactile sensitivity to hugs or clothing type
- Overreaction to smells
- Restricted diet, food type, or presentation (the way food is placed on the plate)
- Fine and or gross motor-skill deficits

School-Related Issues

- Difficulty in situations with less structure
- Transitional problems, difficulties changing from one activity to another
- Misinterpretations
- Object of teasing
- Power struggles
- Anxiety issues

Neuropsychiatric Disorders

Tourette Syndrome (TS): This is a disorder of motor and phonic tics. Tics are involuntary complex motor or vocal productions that can be voluntarily suppressed for a time, often associated with ADHD or obsessive-compulsive disorder.

Fetal Alcohol Syndrome (FAS): The child was exposed in utero to alcohol in sufficient quantity so as to produce typical physical features, as well as characteristic behaviors and learning problems. These children tend to have difficulty with number concepts, are very impulsive and inattentive, lack common sense, and tend to have issues with mood regulation.

Fetal Alcohol Effect (FAE): As above, this less severe syndrome sometimes lacks the physical characteristics and is generally milder in symptoms, behaviors, and deficits.

Fetal Methamphetamine Effect: This can come with a full spectrum of difficulties—hyperactivity, impulsivity, irritability, and mood swings might be some of its manifestations.

Other Neuropsychiatric Disorders

- Disorders due to birth trauma, head injury, stroke, cerebral palsy, etc.
- Degenerative brain diseases (childhood onset dementias, very rare)
- Seizure-related psychoses and mood disorders
- Behavioral effects of metabolic diseases (diabetes, etc.)
- Psychoses, behavioral and mood disorders associated with developmental disorders, autism, Asperger's syndrome (considered part of the autism spectrum), intellectually impaired, brain injury, brain infection

Conclusion

- These disorders are biologic in origin with clear but poorly understood effects on the brain.
- Children must be treated in a bio-psycho-socio-spiritual framework (looking at the whole picture—biological, psychological, sociological, and spiritual aspects).
- Teamwork is essential in order to do the best for these children.

When you are confronted with a special-needs child who has a medical or neurological disability, the first concern is whether you can manage the symptoms in your home or the facility. The level of behaviors and whether or not you can access psychiatric, neurologic, or other medical care can generally determine this.

The second concern would be your own lack of knowledge about a particular disorder. It is important that you obtain what information you can about the disorder and work with medical providers to assist with the proper care of this child. You will likely need to case-manage, making sure the child is seen by appropriate specialists, counselors, therapists, and coordinating appointments. It is also up to the caregiver to make sure the physician's orders are followed and to assess whether interventions are working or not so as to provide feedback to healthcare workers.

When a child sees a counselor, he might need sessions alone without the caregiver present, but sessions together can also be helpful. When the child sees a psychiatrist or other physician, the caregiver must be present to provide necessary input as to how treatment is going and whatever history is available.

Notes

16

Finishing Strong

Caring for children who cannot live in their original home is a ministry. Foster care and adoption are ministries. As we involve ourselves in ministry, we often find that the ministry begins to own us, and we no longer are taking care of our own needs. We start to fall apart sometimes without realizing it. Sometimes, we start pulling away from God, affecting our very important relationship with Him. Those who remain focused on Christ and keep life and ministry in balance will be able to make it through victoriously. When we finish our course, we will then hear those precious words, "Well done, good and faithful servant."

What Is Ministry?

- Service to others according to scriptural parameters
- Expending energy to bring others to Christ, teach them, sustain them, help them through hard times, comfort them, and encourage them to good works

> For we are God's handiwork, created in Christ Jesus to do good works, which God prepared in advance for us to do.
>
> —Ephesians 2:10

Balance in Ministry

Commitment within the Context of Priorities

1. God
2. Family
3. Ministry

Knowing your limitations
Possessing good role definition
It is very important that you strive to do the following:

- Maintain personal and professional boundaries.
- Understand your vulnerability and how Satan can make use of you if you do not stay close to Jesus.
- Claim your strength through the Holy Spirit to complete your tasks.
- Understand processes of attachment and countertransference.

Burnout

Sometimes, caregivers come to a point where it seems quite difficult to carry on. The work seems too much, and the children are beyond their expertise. It seems no longer worthwhile to be in the ministry. It is too much. If you get to this point, you may be in burnout.

Burnout is:

- Emotional exhaustion
- Physical exhaustion
- Energy debt
- Physical neglect
- Spiritual neglect
- Vulnerability to mental illness
- Vulnerability to temptation

Symptoms

- Fatigue
- Decreased concentration and attention
- Decreased creativity
- Irritability
- Anger or rage
- Low tolerance for frustration
- Lack of drive
- Desire to run away (even adults want to run away sometimes!)

Steps to Health

> Those who trust in the Lord are like Mount Zion, which cannot be shaken but endures forever.
>
> —Psalm 125:1

> Anxiety weighs down the heart, but a kind word cheers it up.
>
> —Proverbs 12:25

> A generous man will prosper; whoever refreshes others will be refreshed.
>
> —Proverbs 11:25

> Therefore, since we are surrounded by such a great cloud of witnesses, let us throw off everything that hinders and the sin that so easily entangles. And let us run with perseverance the race marked out for us, fixing our eyes on Jesus, the pioneer and perfecter of faith. For the joy set before him he endured the cross, scorning its shame, and sat down at the right hand of the throne of God.
>
> —Hebrews 12:1–2

> We demolish arguments and every pretension that sets itself up against the knowledge of God, and we take captive every thought to make it obedient to Christ. And we will be ready to punish every act of disobedience, once your obedience is complete.
>
> —2 Corinthians 10:5–6

> Repent, then, and turn to God, so that your sins may be wiped out, that times of refreshing may come from the Lord.
>
> —Acts 3:19

> The apostles gathered around Jesus and reported to him all they had done and taught. Then, because so many people were coming and going that they did not even have a chance to eat, he said to them, "Come with me by yourselves to a quiet place and get some rest."
>
> —Mark 6:30–31

Priorities

1. Time management
2. Restoring regular devotional time
3. Maintaining confidence in God
4. Maintaining good relationships
5. Managing anger and frustration
6. Maintaining a positive attitude
7. Maintaining a positive energy balance

Negative Energy

Many things in normal life can consume a great deal of emotional energy:

Conflict
Dealing with people in general
Lack of sleep
Poor nutrition
Tension, anxiety, worries
Other

STRESS

Seek God: Find ways to connect in prayer and Bible study, associating with God's people in worship and praise.
Talk: Communicate with others, sharing your feelings, troubles, worries, and concerns. Or just talk over a cup of coffee or a meal. Dare to also share your dreams, ideas, and inspirations.
Relax: Find ways to reduce tension—read a book, engage in a hobby, listen to music.
Exercise and Eat Right: Treat your body right—fifteen minutes of exercise three times per week can make a big difference. Change your diet to more healthful choices with less saturated fat, lower carbs, more protein, and lots of fruits and vegetables.
Smile: Look for the humor in life—enjoy a funny story, watch an uplifting movie, or laugh together with someone special.
Sleep: Make sure you get the amount of sleep you personally need. We are all different, but the normal is between six and ten hours per night. Seek professional help if you are not getting restful sleep. Avoid caffeine late in the day, after 3:00 or 4:00 p.m. for most people. Develop good sleep hygiene.

Positive Energy

Seek out things that are positive and that will restore expended energy. To remember what might work, keep in mind the following mnemonic:

What types of activities provide energy restoration for you—exercise, hobbies, watching movies? Establish what works best for you.

Elijah the Burned-Out Prophet

1 Kings 19:1–15

Now Ahab told Jezebel everything Elijah had done and how he had killed all the prophets with the sword. So Jezebel sent a messenger to Elijah to say, "May the gods deal with me, be it ever so severely, if by this time tomorrow I do not make your life like that of one of them."
Elijah was afraid and ran for his life. When he came to Beersheba in Judah, he left his servant there, while he himself went a day's journey into the wilderness. He came to a broom bush, sat down under it and prayed that he might die. "I have

had enough, LORD," he said. "Take my life; I am no better than my ancestors." Then he lay down under the bush and fell asleep.

All at once an angel touched him and said, "Get up and eat." He looked around, and there by his head was some bread baked over hot coals, and a jar of water. He ate and drank and then lay down again.

The angel of the LORD came back a second time and touched him and said, "Get up and eat, for the journey is too much for you." So, he got up and ate and drank. Strengthened by that food, he traveled forty days and forty nights until he reached Horeb, the mountain of God. There he went into a cave and spent the night.

The LORD Appears to Elijah

And the word of the LORD came to him: "What are you doing here, Elijah?"

He replied, "I have been very zealous for the LORD God Almighty. The Israelites have rejected your covenant, torn down your altars, and put your prophets to death with the sword. I am the only one left, and now they are trying to kill me too."

The LORD said, "Go out and stand on the mountain in the presence of the LORD, for the LORD is about to pass by."

Then a great and powerful wind tore the mountains apart and shattered the rocks before the LORD, but the LORD was not in the wind. After the wind there was an earthquake, but the LORD was not in the earthquake. After the earthquake came a fire, but the LORD was not in the fire. And after the fire came a gentle whisper. When Elijah heard it, he pulled his cloak over his face and went out and stood at the mouth of the cave.

Then a voice said to him, "What are you doing here, Elijah?"

He replied, "I have been very zealous for the LORD God Almighty. The Israelites have rejected your covenant, torn down your altars, and put your prophets to death with the sword. I am the only one left, and now they are trying to kill me too."

The LORD said to him, "Go back the way you came, and go to the Desert of Damascus. When you get there, anoint Hazael king over Aram. Also, anoint Jehu son of Nimshi king over Israel, and anoint Elisha son of Shaphat from Abel Meholah to succeed you as prophet. Jehu will put to death any who escape the sword of Hazael, and Elisha will put to death any who escape the sword of Jehu. Yet I reserve seven thousand in Israel—all whose knees have not bowed down to Baal and whose mouths have not kissed him."

Elijah had a very hard job ministering to a people who would not listen. He came to a point after a literal spiritual mountain-top experience (see preceding chapter in 1 Kings), that he was burned-out, doubting God and needing restoration. What was the process that God used? He first provided sleep and then food, sleep and then food. When he was physically restored, then God worked on restoring him spiritually. God answered for him the question of who He, God, really is. Not the powerful wind, not the earthquake, not the fire, but the still small voice. Once he was able to realize His presence, God restored him to the job he needed to do. The recipe still works for us today. We need to get the physical rest and restoration, place God back on His throne, and get back to serving Him with all of our hearts.

Keeping balance in our lives will help to prevent the burnout, but even then, as in the case of Elijah, sometimes, the burden is too much, we just need to retreat and let God restore us back to full function.

Maintaining Healthy Boundaries

An easy way to burn out and cause damage to those you are ministering to is to not observe appropriate boundaries. Many of the children we work with who are placed in out-of-home situations are sexualized and thus do not have well-established boundaries.

Boundaries in these children were redefined by abuse. Attachment and emotional closeness are confused with sexual arousal. To be accepted, they feel there must be a sexual component. They have a great deal of difficulty with unconditional love.

As outlined in the material on Structure (see chapter 2), a functioning system must have well-defined roles and responsibilities. Living and working within our defined roles reduces burnout and other problems.

Remember the Role of Caregiver:

- Provide structure.
- Be a listening ear.
- Provide encouragement, correction, direction.
- Assure that basic needs are met in a timely fashion.
- Be a mentor and example.

The Role of Caregiver Is Not These:

- Rescuer
- Intimate Confidant
- Therapist
- Adoptive Parent
- Doctor

Review of Transference and Countertransference

Transference: The child transfers to the therapist or caregiver attributes of an important individual in his or her past.

Countertransference: The caregiver transfers attributes of someone important in his or her own past onto the child.

The child might see you as the hated mother who abandoned him in the past and react to you in a hateful way. This might result in verbal and physical aggression and difficulty forming a relationship until it is worked through.

You might see in the child something from your past that causes you to react from the subconscious in a way that is not beneficial to the child (for example, overreacting to a report of sexual abuse, due to your own childhood abuse you experienced).

Understanding of this concept and continually examining ourselves to determine our own motives and why we react in certain ways serves to help us connect better and to keep ourselves safe from boundary violations and reduces our own anger and frustration.

Approaches to Keep Us Going

Be humble, and learn from your mistakes.

Be able to laugh at yourself when appropriate.

Constantly analyze your own reactions to see where they are coming from. Learn the history of each child so you have some understanding of why he or she might react in a certain way to specific approaches.

> If any of you lacks wisdom, you should ask of God, who gives generously to all without finding fault, and it will be given to you.
>
> —James 1:5

Our Mission

> Therefore, my dear brothers and sisters, stand firm. Let nothing move you. Always give yourselves fully to the work of the Lord, because you know that your labor in the Lord is not in vain.
>
> —1 Corinthians 15:58

Children's Ministry

Working with children is one of the most challenging and important ministries. Burnout among childcare workers is among the highest of any type of ministry. Stress in the work environment, family, emotional turmoil, and conflicts are all very frequent and can be intense if you are not caring for yourself physically and spiritually. These will be a constant drain on our energy.

Finding Success in Ministry

- Why are you here—to love unconditionally, strengthen your character, or live in service for God's children?
- What are your personal and spiritual goals?
- What are your goals in ministry?
- What is your mission statement?

Remember, you are here for the children. Attachment is a two-way street that is stressful for both parties involved, so do not let it carry you away. Boundaries are set for very good reasons and must be observed for your personal, physical, and spiritual safety.

Priorities

1. Jesus and you
2. Family
3. Ministry
4. Your personal desires

Make use of the worksheet on the following page to assist you in developing a balance in your ministry, to provide some guidance in focusing your direction and purpose, and to help you not just survive this difficult ministry but to thrive and *finish strong!*

Summary and Action Plan

Explore this for yourself and write why you are in this ministry. If your motives need to be corrected, ask God to help you correct them.

- What is my personal mission statement?
- What are my motives to be in this ministry?
- What are my goals in this ministry for five years from now?
- What are the negatives in my life and ministry: those things that consume energy?
- What are the positives in my life: things I can do to gain or restore energy?
- Using the STRESS mnemonic, how can I balance my life and ministry?

Notes

17

Spiritual Warfare

It is very easy to ignore the reality of the spiritual world and just go on with what we can see and feel, hear and touch. However, the reality is far different. One of the best tricks of the evil one is to make us ignore the reality of his existence so he catches us off guard. Many of the children who come into care come from incredible backgrounds of evil and depravity. So many of the stories I have heard over the years could not even be printed here. If a child is exposed to evil, there exists the possibility of demonization. We have to be aware of this but not be looking for a demon behind every door. Spiritual Warfare basically has to do with how we battle against the forces of evil that have captivated many of our children.

What Is Reality?

- Do you only believe in what you can experience with five senses? There is more!
- You are not a body that has a soul but rather *a soul that just happens to have a body.*
- You are an eternal being locked in time and space for a bit.
- Reality extends beyond the visible.
- The Bible describes an entire universe we cannot comprehend.

- We easily accept the reality of the Holy Spirit, but some have problems with the idea that evil spirits still exist.
- Fundamentally, nothing has changed from the time Jesus walked the earth. We have cars, electricity, and nicer houses, but…
- People still sin, they are still in need of a savior, and evil still resides in the earth.
- This is not the same world God created and said, "It is good." Something happened to the Creation when Adam sinned.

The Healing of Two Demon-Possessed Men

> When he arrived at the other side in the region of the Gadarenes, two demon-possessed men coming from the tombs met him. They were so violent that no one could pass that way. "What do you want with us, Son of God?" they shouted. "Have you come here to torture us before the appointed time?"
> Some distance from them a large herd of pigs was feeding. The demons begged Jesus, "If you drive us out, send us into the herd of pigs." He said to them, "Go!" So, they came out and went into the pigs, and the whole herd rushed down the steep bank into the lake and died in the water. Those tending the pigs ran off, went into the town and reported all this, including what had happened to the demon-possessed men. Then the whole town went out to meet Jesus. And when they saw him, they pleaded with him to leave their region.
>
> —Matthew 8:28–34

The Battle Is Spiritual

> The Spirit clearly says that in later times some will abandon the faith and follow deceiving spirits and things taught by demons. Such teachings come through hypocritical liars, whose consciences have been seared as with a hot iron.
>
> —1 Timothy 4:1–2

The Battle Is Against a Kingdom

> For our struggle is not against flesh and blood, but against the rulers, against the authorities, against the powers of this dark world and against the spiritual forces of evil in the heavenly realms.
>
> —Ephesians 6:12 (NIV), ***daimonizomai*** (δαιμονίζομαι)

The only word used for demonic involvement in scripture. It could be translated: *Demonization*

Modern-Day Demonization

> Nothing has changed, demons still wander the earth, Satan still seeks whom he may destroy: Be alert and of sober mind. Your enemy the devil prowls around like a roaring lion looking for someone to devour.
>
> —1 Peter 5:8

Taking a Spiritual History

- Circumstances of growing up
- Religious orientation of family
- Experiences with the occult (Ouija, new ageism, animism, Satanism, etc.)
- Involvement in a cult (communes, spiritualism, animism, traditional religions such as native Hawaiian or Santeria in Mexico)
- Deliberate dealings with the devil
- Pornography, especially gay, bestial, extreme perversions
- Is there a personal commitment to Christ?
- What are the current temptations and difficulties?
- Are there mental-health problems and/or addictions
- Voices in the head or outside
- Visions of evil characters
- Aversion to the Bible, discomfort in church
- Anger or discomfort at the mention of the Blood of Christ

Demonization

- A fairly common phenomenon worldwide.
- Occurs at various levels.
- Some demons leave upon baptism.
- Some persist and have more power and authority.
- All are dangerous to the unaware and inexperienced.
- Spiritual damage or even physical harm can occur if one tries to deal with the demons without knowing how to approach.

- As God's kingdom is very organized, angels have rank and authority as seen through the scriptures.
- God's people who are filled with His Spirit have power and authority over these spiritual beings.

  For I am convinced that neither death nor life, neither angels nor demons, neither the present nor the future, nor any powers, neither height nor depth, nor anything else in all creation, will be able to separate us from the love of God that is in Christ Jesus our Lord.

  —Romans 8:38–39

- Angels, principalities, powers—a hierarchy of authority
- Some quite a bit more powerful than others

Preparing for Battle

If it is determined that someone is in need of warfare to deal with the demonic:

- Prepare yourself, releasing anything that might hinder your relationship with God.
- Have at least two other experienced mature Christians to assist.
- Pray for protection.
- Having others outside the room praying can also help.

Authority of the Believer We Have:

The authority given us by Jesus and through the power of His blood:

- Authority to command angels
- Authority to command evil spirits to depart

Evil spirits can be very resistive and powerful; battle might take hours or even separate sessions to complete the task. Remember, it is about His power ***not*** our own.

The process begins with opening in prayer and then directly addressing the demon. Sometimes, there is a response in the voice of the counselee, sometimes in another voice; sometimes (most often), there is minimal response until the process moves forward. The demon can be commanded to leave in the name of Jesus and by the authority of His blood. Sometimes, the battle begins at this point with refusal, arguing, and defiance. The individual may have some emotional response, such as crying or experiencing pain. Command the demon to stop causing the pain or discomfort and to leave. It might take quite some time, and there might be more than one. Those not in direct confrontation must continue to pray. The leader continues to command, by authority, that the demon depart. Some are quite powerful and might take more than one visit. One important part is to continually ask the individual if he is willing to let go of the demon. Some do not wish to release this companion who has been with him for many years. Once there is a willingness, then proceed with commanding until it is completed. This is only an example of the way I have managed situations; other mature believers might have other effective scripture-based ways to proceed.

Case History

José Luis was a seven-year-old child when brought by relatives to the orphanage in Mexico City, as his parents no longer were able to care for him. He initially adjusted fairly well but then started having episodes in which he was not coherent, only repeating, "I have to go now." On one occasion, he was let go and allowed to get up. He walked right out of the facility where a woman was waiting to take him, having presumably been summoned by the demons herself. It was not known who she was; she just came out of an alley intent on taking Jose Luis from me. I had to wrestle him away from her; she was very strong and had the same one-hundred-mile stare the child had. Once he was brought back, we prayed with him and repeatedly commanded the evil spirits to leave. He calmed considerably, and we felt that the battle, though not over, was making some progress. It was noted he had a *Y*-shaped scar on his head that he stated was from a beating he suffered at the hand of his father or mother, possibly from an iron or a belt. The story kept changing. One day, he came on his own to the clinic, asking to have his *Y* removed. He recalled having been branded by his parents in a special ceremony where there were candles and everyone was in black robes. The *Y* represented the first initial of his priestly name. With several people assigned to pray on the outside of the clinic, the *Y* was carefully removed and the wound sutured. He felt much more freedom after that and grew rapidly in his faith. One day, while camping in the forest with his group home, some unseen force threw him off a cliff into standing water while he was hiking with the others. He was OK for a while, but then had breathing problems. By the time he was brought to the clinic, his condition was very serious. While in the process of preparing to take him to the hospital, he passed away. Resuscitation efforts were in vain. This had an unexpected outcome, as the spirits seemed to have a stronghold on him. His parents showed up about a year later to take him back—it was presumed he had been selected to be a satanic priest. Instead, God had victory and took the boy home.

His peers always called him Champion, which was how he was remembered during his memorial service.

The above true story is mentioned so as to give a perspective of the seriousness of the real spiritual battle that is going on all of the time for these children. These children belong to God, and we must battle for them to reclaim them and to bring them back. We must be aware of the spiritual nature of the battle and take care that the enemy does not deceive us.

Our battles can be more than just individual children. There are times when sit-uations in the home come to a point of spiritual danger or oppression in the home that the staff need to engage in battle to remove the negative influence and call upon angels for special protection and help. If we think in spiritual terms, we can be much better prepared to battle spiritual forces and keep our children safe and close to God.

Conclusion

- We are in a spiritual battle.
- Though not all evil comes from demons, they are real and active in the world today.
- Their activity will intensify as the end of the age approaches.
- We must be aware and ready to battle when necessary.
- The believer has authority to cast out demons and to make use of angels in the course of our work.

Our Daily Commission

> Put on the full armor of God, so that you can take your stand against the devil's schemes. For our struggle is not against flesh and blood, but against the rulers, against the authorities, against the powers of this dark world and against the spiritual forces of evil in the heavenly realms. Therefore, put on the full armor of God, so that when the day of evil comes, you may be able to stand your ground, and after you have done everything, to stand. Stand firm then, with the belt of truth buckled around your waist, with the breastplate of righteousness in place, and with your feet fitted with the readiness that comes from the gospel of peace. In addition to all this, take up the shield of faith, with which you can extinguish all the flaming arrows of the evil one. Take the helmet of salvation and the sword of the Spirit, which is the word of God. And pray in the Spirit on all occasions with all kinds of prayers and requests. With this in mind, be alert and always keep on praying for all the Lord's people.
>
> —Ephesians 6:11–18

Notes

18

Suicidal and Self-Destructive Behavior

One of the very tragic situations is that of a child who comes to the point of committing suicide. I have dealt with children who were suicidal from age four on upward. I have had to help put back together families devastated by the suicide of a child. As caregivers, it is vital that you are very familiar with the signs of a child who is in deep distress and might be considering ending his or her life. You also need to know how to properly respond so as to not make things worse but to bring them back from the brink and help them to live.

Why Suicide?

Why does a child come to the point that he or she seriously considers ending their life? These are some possible causes:

- Hopelessness
- Overwhelmed, feeling trapped

- Confusion
- Romantic breakup
- Death of a close loved one
- Accidental (playing with dangerous objects, driving too fast, etc.)
- Depression
- Psychosis
- Low serotonin levels in brain
- Emotional distress
- Physical pain that becomes intolerable
- Abandonment
- A sense that no one loves or cares for him or her
- Overwhelming psychiatric or medical symptoms
- Combinations of the above, mainly depression

Suicidal Risk

The risk for suicidal behavior is increased in those who have the following:

- Long-standing mental or physical illness
- Poor connections with others for emotional support
- Lack of future orientation (goals, purpose)
- Isolative behavior
- Incidental statements that could be taken to mean there are thoughts of suicide: "I'm not sure I should be around" or "Nobody would miss me" or "I am no good to anyone," in the context of other risk factors

Those at risk might exhibit these behaviors:

- Sudden change in behavior, suddenly happy or relieved, giving things away, becoming quite isolated, and not communicating
- Change in sleep patterns
- Drawings or writings that are dark, bloody, self-deprecating, or reflecting self-hatred
- Obsession with weapons when not a prior obsession
- Discussing with others ways to commit suicide

The suicidal child might also show these characteristics:

- Preoccupation about death or suicide, such as talking about death, looking up ways to die on Internet, or texting about it on the phone or social media.
- Prior history of attempts
- Current diagnosis of major depression, bipolar disorder, panic disorder, schizophrenia, or PTSD
- Self-cutting
- Increase in established self-injurious behavior (SIB) patterns in a child who is able to understand death
- A relative or close friend has attempted or succeeded with suicide

Suicide and RAD

- Reactive attachment disorder (RAD), unresolved, leaves the child with poor ability to connect to others for emotional support.
- Life seems overwhelming, and social expectations are stressful.
- There is confusion about loyalties: "With whom can I attach?" or "Will my past attachments allow it?"
- This child might be very sensitive to criticism, as self-esteem is not well developed.
- Many RAD kids are genetically predisposed to mental illness.
- Untreated mental illness in a parent might have produced the environment leading to the attachment problems.
- Coping skills are generally not well developed, and there is little trust in others.
- To fill the void, the child might develop self-injury patterns that predispose to eventual suicidal behavior.

Assessment

- What is the child's level of function, IQ, or other measure? If mental age is five or less, the child might not understand the concept of death or its permanence.
- Is there an existing physical illness, chronic condition, or pain?
- What about previously diagnosed mental illness?
- Are there any changes in sleep patterns or behavior?

- Have there been prior threats of suicide? Some suicidal individuals follow the "law of diminishing returns" progression—from threats to scratching to cutting to overdosing to shooting self.

Approaches

Once history is ascertained, a face-to-face interview with staff will occur. Take a nonjudgmental, passive, friendly, compassionate approach. Ask whether the child feels like hurting himself, why, what would be different if he did commit suicide, and how he would do it (in detail). Determine at this point whether the threat is realistic and whether the child has access to his or her intended means for carrying it out. Even if the child is convinced that three aspirin will kill him, consider it a serious threat.

Through questioning, one of the following is determined:

- Immediate danger to self, even if closely monitored
- Immediate danger to self, but can be safe with close monitoring
- No immediate danger, but patterns developing in which dangerous behaviors are likely in the future
- No immediate danger, a situational stress, so threats to self were only of the moment

Intervention

Immediate Danger to Self, Even If Closely Monitored

- If threats are to the point that there is imminent danger, the individual cannot resolve the issue, and the child remains intent on self-destruction, then hospitalization is necessary if that is an option.
- If you cannot obtain confinement in a secure place, one-to-one staffing is necessary until a physician or psychiatrist evaluates the child.
- If the hospital is unable to admit him or her, an emergency-room physician, in consultation with the facility's psychiatric staff or the psychiatrist on call, can provide medication to calm the patient for a safe passage home, where close monitoring can be put in place.
- Priority is containment until he or she can be brought back to a level of safety.

Immediate Danger to Self, But Can Be Safe with Close Monitoring

- Clear the living area of unsafe materials, medications, sharp objects, break-able objects, heavy objects, cords or string, and belts. Girls might need to give up their bras if threats include hanging.
- One-to-one or two-to-one staffing should be put in place until the situation is deemed safe.
- Immediately consult with a psychiatric consultant or physician to determine if medications are necessary.
- Provide supervision, but do not provide undue attention so as to reward the behavior.
- Provide counseling to de-escalate and provide alternatives to suicidal behaviors.
- With assistance of a counselor, work to reduce the supervision as the patient takes responsibility for herself.

No Immediate Danger, But Patterns Developing in Which Dangerous Behaviors Are Likely in the Future

- Provide counseling for the child to develop coping skills and strategies to manage stress.
- Take care to not over- or underreact.
- Avoid creating a reward scenario—attention, even negative, is a major reward.
- Arrange for a psychiatric consultation as soon as possible.

No Immediate Danger; Situational Stress, So Threats to Self Were Only of the Moment

- Talk through the situation, mostly listening and allowing the child to safely vent.
- Once passion has cleared, begin a dialogue regarding better ways to deal with stress.

Chronic Suicidal Behaviors

- Ongoing counseling and psychiatric care are needed.
- With the help of a counselor or psychiatrist, determine at what level of threat which types of interventions should be undertaken.
- All threats are taken seriously, but response is graded as to what would be most helpful.

- Some children cannot relinquish the suicidal behavior and will require secure, long-term placement.

Summary

- All suicide threats are communicating something and must be responded to.
- Depending on the level of the threat, intervention ranges from inpatient or institutional care to crisis counseling for a few sessions or even just resolving the immediate crisis.
- When in doubt, head to the hospital—the emergency-room staff can help you evaluate.
- If the child is a danger to him or herself and refuses to go to the hospital, call on the police to help.

Notes

19

Administration of Medication

Many children in care will either come with medications or be prescribed them while in care. Some are for the short term, while others are for months or years to deal with a chronic condition. In order to safely administer the proper medications, there are several items of importance:

- Learn the name of the medication, what it is for, and its possible side effects. It is also very important to know whether the child is allergic to particular medications and that such information is available to all caregivers and medical providers who work with the child. If you have Internet access and information was not provided by the physician, WebMD.com is a very reliable source run by Medscape.
- Learn the "five rights of medication administration":

  1. **The *right* medication:** Does it match what the doctor said it is supposed to be?

2. **The *right* dose:** Is it a half pill, one pill, two pills, a teaspoon, or a tablespoon?
3. **The *right* patient:** Does the name on the medicine container match the name of the child to whom you are administering it?
4. **The *right* time:** Should it be administered morning, noon, night, a specific time of the day, after a particular meal, or not with food or milk?
5. **The *right* route:** Is it administered orally, by injection, rectally, under the tongue, in the nose, or topically?

- To administer the medication, remove the required quantity from the bottle and place in either the hand of the patient or a disposable cup. Have the patient place the medication in the mouth; in the case of pills, provide water, unless it's a sublingual pill not requiring such.
- With liquid, pour into the measuring cup or withdraw with a syringe that is provided with the medication, taking care to measure the exact quantity required. If it is given from a syringe, place in one side of the mouth and push slowly; with a measuring cup, allow the patient to administer if old enough to handle the cup.
- Make sure the medication is swallowed. If you're not sure, have the patient open his mouth and move the tongue about to see if the pill or liquid remains.
- In the United States and other more developed areas, medication can be packaged in bubble packs with one month of medication in the pack, each pack for one medication, given at one time in the day. These can be stored according to whether morning, noon, or night and under the name of the patient. This type of packaging can help keep track of medications.
- In the case of smaller facilities or foster/adoptive homes with a few children with more than one medication administered each day, a med set can be pre-pared on a weekly basis in which the medications are placed carefully in the appropriate sections for each day of the week and each time of day. At time of administration, the appropriate section is opened and medications placed in the disposable cup, which is then provided to the patient, who is observed taking the medication.
- Topical medications generally do not have a dosage. A small quantity is placed on the gloved hand of the one administering the medication and rubbed thoroughly on the affected area.
- Patches are placed on a clean, dry area of skin away from the location of the prior patch and, in the case of small children, not reachable by their hands.

- Medication that dissolves under the tongue is to be given without water, and no liquid is given for about ten minutes.
- Injectable medication is to be administered only by qualified medical personnel. Some injectables might be stored on site before an appointment with a medical provider who administers or the arrival of trained personnel (nurse, physician, etc.) to administer. In locations without medical personnel, care-givers can be trained to provide injections.
- Some medications are addictive and considered controlled substances in most locations. Much care should be taken to keep these medications in a secure location. This includes stimulants for hyperactive children, strong pain medications, and antianxiety meds.
- There must be a secure location away from access by the children in which the medication can be safely stored and organized—a locked storage box, cupboard, closet, or special room. Make sure that if refrigeration is required, medication is stored in a section of the refrigerator where it can be easily accessed by staffers but not by children.

First-Aid Kit

Each home should have a first-aid kit consisting of material for basic wound care and safe over-the-counter (nonprescription) medication commonly used in house-holds for the treatment of minor illnesses.

Suggested Contents

- Bandages
- Gauze
- Tape
- Triple-antibiotic ointment
- Hydrogen peroxide
- Acetaminophen (Panadol, Tylenol, etc.) liquid and tablets
- Ibuprofen tablets and liquid
- Cough syrup containing guaifenesin and dextromethorphan
- Loperamide liquid and tablets for treating diarrhea
- Other items as appropriate and locally available

Follow exactly what the package states regarding the dosage for a particular weight and age of the child. In many locations, a local physician needs to review the medication and sign off on the dosages and quantity of items in the kit.

Proper use of medication can be very helpful in alleviating symptoms and treating many diseases. On the flip side, medications can be very dangerous if used in dosages that are inappropriate or in cases of allergies to the medication.

It is very important that the above guidelines be strictly observed in the usage of medication so as to avoid complications and to assure that particular disease states and disorders are properly treated or managed, with the goal of keeping the children healthy and developing normally.

You can copy and post the "five rights," located on the next page, to assist in remembering the principles of administration of medication.

The Five Rights of Medication Administration

1. The Right Medication: Does it match what the doctor said it is supposed to be?
2. The Right Dose: Is it a half pill, one pill, two pills, a teaspoon, or a tablespoon? Read the label.
3. The Right Patient: Does the name on the medicine container match the name of the child to whom you are administering it?
4. The Right Time: Should it be administered morning, noon, night, a specific time of the day, after a particular meal, with food or milk, or not with food or milk?
5. The Right Route: Is it administered orally, by injection, rectally, under the tongue, in the nose, or topically?

Notes

Bibliography

American Psychiatric Association. 2013 The Diagnostic and Statistical Manual of Mental Disorders (DSM-5). 5th ed. Washington DC: American Psychiatric Press, 2013 Anderson, Neil T. 1990. The Bondage Breaker: Overcoming Negative Thoughts, Irrational Feelings, Habitual Sins. Eugene OR Harvest House Publishing.

Bowlby, John. 1988 A Secure Base: Parent-Child Attachment and Healthy Human Development New York Basic Books.

Cline, Foster, and Jim Fay. 1990 Parenting with Love and Logic. Colorado Springs, CO: Pinon Press.

Hughes, Daniel A. 1997 Facilitating Developmental Attachment: The Road to Emotional Recovery and Behavioral Change in Foster and Adopted Children. Northvale NJ. Jason Aronson Inc.

Mahler, Margaret S. Fred Pine, and Anni Bergman. 1975. The Psychological Birth of the Human Infant: Symbiosis and Individuation. New York Basic Books.

Smalley, Gary, and John Trent. 1986. The Blessing. Nashville TN Thomas Nelson Publishing.

Psychol Bull. 2018 May; 144(5): 532–555.

Published online 2018 Mar 1. doi: 10.1037/bul0000141

A Meta-Analysis of Longitudinal Associations between Substance Use and Interpersonal Attachment Security Catherine Fairbairn, Daniel A. Briley, Dahyeon Kang, R. Chris Fraley, Benjamin L. Hankin, and Talia Ariss

Websites

MentalHelp.net

Use the site's search window to find information regarding the many diagnoses of mental disorders in children.

Aspergers.com

The Asperger's Disorder Homepage offers information and resources.

ninds.nih.gov

The National Institute of Neurological Disorders and Strokes has information regarding autism spectrum, attention deficit, learning disorders, and other child-hood neurologic syndromes.

About the Author

Larry Banta was born and raised in Ohio, on a farm near Cincinnati. Upon graduating high school in Lebanon, Ohio, he left for college in Lincoln, Nebraska, where he obtained a BS in microbiology. From there, he attended University of Nebraska Medical College, where he was awarded his MD degree.

During his junior year in college, everything changed for him when he accepted Christ into his life. He soon met and married Ellen Fairbrother, a missionary kid from India. The two shared a passion for children and for missions. On a *Reader's Digest* Medical Assistance Program scholarship, he was able to complete the last three months of medical school at an orphanage in India, where he was introduced to foreign missions. During the couple's time in India, Ellen started a preschool, while Larry helped design a mission hospital and assess local medical needs.

With plans to return to India following medical training, Larry completed an internship in internal medicine and completed two years of general practice in South Dakota. Efforts were made to return to India to work with Hanson's disease, but missionary visas for doctors were not being approved at that time. Instead, the family headed to Kenya for a twenty-month tour in which the first year was post-famine rehabilitation work among the Pokot tribe located in Kiwawa, West Pokot. The second year was spent in Central Kenya in the Samburu District, establishing a church and a clinic. Due to health issues, it was necessary to return to US in 1984.

It was with feelings of failure and discouragement that the Bantas returned to the United States. While Larry prayed during the flight back, it became evident that God was leading them in a particular direction—psychiatry. At first, the calling did not seem to make sense, as they deeply desired to serve on the foreign mission field, and psychiatry had not made it there yet. On arrival in the United States, they were privileged to stay with retired missionaries Norton and Lois Bare, Ellen's grandparents. Both were elderly, and Norton suffered from Alzheimer's disease. He was a retired psychiatrist, however. With no apparent knowledge of Larry's time with God in route, Norton took all his recent psychiatric journals and psychiatric newsletters to the couch, where they waited in a nice pile for Larry's arrival. Prior to and subsequent to the time he placed them on the couch and announced, "These are for Larry, he needs them," he had not many other words that made any sense. It was his final service for God, apparently.

Seeing the collection on the couch was the turning point—there was no doubt what God desired for Larry. He called a professor from medical school and had a training position within a few minutes.

Following general psychiatry residency, Larry completed a fellowship in child and adolescent psychiatry. During training, he was introduced to working with foster parents and out-of-home-placed special-needs children, specifically with those who had attachment disorders.

During the next few years, following completion of training, Larry made efforts to connect with children's ministries. As a family, the Bantas traveled to Haiti. This opened many doors, and it became evident that psychiatric care had something to offer. They were invited back to Haiti annually for several years. During that time, they were able to make contact with Niños de Mexico, a Christian home for children in Mexico City. On inquiry, the administration became excited about a visit from a psychiatrist and wanted to learn what might help.

Larry and Ellen soon started making regular trips to Mexico to train personnel, evaluate children, and provide assistance with the organization as a whole. Ellen wondered if it would be a good idea to move there to offer more assistance, so they served there on site from 1996 through 1999 and as consultants until 2006. Larry started a clinic to serve the medical and psychiatric needs of the children.

In late 2017, Ellen passed away after a long battle with multiple sclerosis. Larry remarried to Evelyn, who is a licensed professional counselor. They work together on various projects related to mental health and children's ministry.

It is their prayer that this manual would be widely distributed and serve to encourage and help those who work with these special children. Larry and Evelyn are available for speaking and training on these and other topics and can be contacted via e-mail: evnlar19@gmail.com